Throughout the nineteenth century, American fiction displayed a fascination with women's speech – describing how women's voices sound and what reactions their speech produces, especially in their male listeners. Closer inspection of these recurring descriptions reveals that they also performed political work that has had a profound – though until now unspecified – impact on American culture.

Caroline Levander illustrates how commentaries on the female voice, propounded by such writers as Henry James, William Dean Howells, and Noah Webster, played a central role in attempts to define and enforce the radical social changes instituted by the emerging bourgeoisie. Levander also shows how nineteenth-century women authors depicted the female voice as a central theme in their novels and how these portrayals affected public speech.

With her careful analysis of the relation between speech and voice, Levander makes an intriguing and important contribution to the ongoing effort of literary scholars and cultural historians to redefine nineteenth-century American political culture and the role of women within it.

CAMBRIDGE STUDIES IN AMERICAN LITERATURE
AND CULTURE

Voices of the Nation

CAMBRIDGE STUDIES IN AMERICAN LITERATURE AND CULTURE

Editor: Eric Sundquist, *University of California, Los Angeles*

Founding Editor: Albert Gelpi, *Stanford University*

Advisory Board

Nina Baym, *University of Illinois, Urbana-Champaign*
Sacvan Bercovitch, *Harvard University*
Albert Gelpi, *Stanford University*
Myra Jehlen, *Rutgers University*
Carolyn Porter, *University of California, Berkeley*
Robert Stepto, *Yale University*
Tony Tanner, *King's College, Cambridge University*

Books in the series

(Continued on page following index.)

Voices of the Nation

Women and Public Speech in Nineteenth-Century American Literature and Culture

CAROLINE FIELD LEVANDER

Trinity University

CAMBRIDGE
UNIVERSITY PRESS

PUBLISHED BY THE PRESS SYNDICATE OF THE UNIVERSITY OF CAMBRIDGE
The Pitt Building, Trumpington Street, Cambridge CB2 1RP, United Kingdom

CAMBRIDGE UNIVERSITY PRESS
The Edinburgh Building, Cambridge CB2 2RU, United Kingdom
40 West 20th Street, New York, NY 10011-4211, USA
10 Stamford Road, Oakleigh, Melbourne 3166, Australia

First published 1998

Printed in the United States of America

Typeset in Baskerville

Library of Congress Cataloging-in-Publication Data
Levander, Caroline Field, 1964–
Voices of the nation : women and public speech in nineteenth-
century American literature and culture / Caroline Field Levander.
p. cm. – (Cambridge studies in American literature and
culture ; 114)
Revision of author's thesis (Ph. D.) – Trinity University.
Includes bibliographical references (p.   ) and index.
ISBN 0-521-59374-3 (hb)
1. American fiction – 19th century – History and criticism.
2. Women and literature – United States – History – 19th century.
3. American fiction – Women authors – History and criticism.
4. Public speaking for women – History – 19th century.   5. Public
speaking for women in literature.   6. Oratory in literature.
7. Speech in literature.   8. Voice in literature.   9. Women in
literature.   I. Title.   II. Series.
PS374.W6L48   1997
813'.309352042 – dc21   97-24281
                                                              CIP

A catalog record for this book is available from the British Library.

ISBN 0 521 59374 3 hardback

For Alan

Contents

CONTENTS

Acknowledgments

This book would not have been possible without the generous support of many people. I owe my greatest intellectual debt to David Minter, whose tireless attention over the years to the arguments driving this book and to the prose with which I've made them has strengthened the final product incalculably. I am also greatly indebted to the wonderful intellectual support of Scott Derrick, Helena Michie, Eric Sundquist, Eileen Cleere, Stephen De Silva, Barbara Ladner, and Rebecca Stern. Heather Sullivan, Kris Boudreau, Willis Salomon, Philip Weinstein, Mark Field, Michele Vobach, and Karen Flack offered generous intellectual and emotional support as this project neared completion, while Mary Racine, Grant Morrison, and Janet Brown, with their editorial help, made completion possible. For their enthusiastic willingness to listen to parts of this project and to provide a congenial home away from home on my research trips to Boston, I thank Meg, Jes, and Emily Mandel. Very special thanks go to my parents, Charles and Germaine Field, for instilling the love of books that made writing one of my own possible, and for all of their encouragement along the way. Finally, for his profound belief in me and his unfailing commitment to my intellectual life, I owe my deepest debt of gratitude to Alan Levander.

This book owes much to institutions as well as to individuals. Without the generous support of Rice University and Trinity University, *Voices of the Nation* would have been much longer in the making. The Lodieska Stockbridge Vaughan Dissertation Fellowship allowed me uninterrupted time to complete my dissertation, while the Gene Northrup Faculty Research Fellowship provided me with time to revise it. Trinity has provided ongoing financial support for this project, for which I am truly appreciative. Finally, for providing permission to reprint "Bawdy Talk: The Politics of Women's Public Speech in *The Lecturess* and *The Bostonians*," I thank *American Literature*, in which a slightly different version of this essay appeared in September 1995.

Introduction

Gender, Speech, and Nineteenth-Century American Life

─────────

... the bright, up darting flame of her talk rose and fell like an improvisation on the keys ... it's the voice, you know – the enchanting voice! ... Its richness was quite independent of the words she might pronounce.

Henry James, *The Tragic Muse* (1890)

She had a slow, quaint way of talking, that seemed a pleasant personal modification of some ancestral Yankee drawl, and her voice was low and cozy.... She never says anything you can remember; nothing in flashes or ripples ... but [has] a sort of droll way of looking at things.

William Dean Howells, *The Rise of Silas Lapham* (1885)

... her voice gave a curious charm to [his] old favorites when she read them; and many hours he listened contentedly to the voice whose youth made Montaigne's worldly wisdom seem the shrewder; whose music gave a certain sweetness to Voltaire's bitter wit ... whose pitying wonder added pathos to the melancholy brilliancy of De Quincey.

Louisa May Alcott, *A Modern Mephistopheles* (1866)

As in the three passages just quoted, the sound of women's speech is featured throughout the pages of nineteenth-century American fiction. Beginning with Charles Brockden Brown's *Wieland* (1798) and extending into the early twentieth century with F. Scott Fitzgerald's *The Great Gatsby* (1925), American novels devote much space to describing how women's voices sound and what reactions women's

1

speech produces, especially in their male listeners. Depictions of men's intense interest in women's pleasing and distinct utterances occur with a frequency that initially seems to reinforce the idea – prevalent in middle-class American culture since its inception – that "essential," and therefore unalterable, differences distinguish men from women.[1] But in the following chapters I argue that closer inspection of this persistent imagining of women's "natural" linguistic difference,[2] in nonliterary as well as in literary texts, reveals, not its inevitability, but rather its constructed, strategic, and crucial role in the dramatic social transformation that the nation underwent in the nineteenth century. Thus, I seek to show that, far from surfacing within American literary and cultural texts as merely descriptive passages, the lengthy, detailed, recurring depictions of women's voices that I examine do political work that had a profound, though as yet unspecified, impact on American culture. In order to describe the political burden that American writing placed on women's language, I explore, in the first part of the book, the commentaries about the female voice that helped the nation understand and represent itself as it was transformed by the emergence of a new and increasingly powerful middle class. With that description as a context, I then examine the subsequent impact of these commentaries on women's ability to speak within the "separate spheres" that were this class's primary construct and, in so doing, develop new ways of thinking about the public significance of women's speech in an evolving political arena.

That political arena became increasingly defined by and identified with the changing speech of its male members, as the United States reordered itself both physically and ideologically around sharply differentiated "public" and "private" spheres. As men left the rural communities of America and Europe in increasing numbers and moved into the American marketplace,[3] they influenced and finally transformed the language spoken there. By producing, according to their interpreters, an "especially vigorous . . . public debate"[4] that reflected their particular interests and attitudes, these relocated citizens helped to make the United States famous for the quality of speech around which its political life was structured. In his 1864 memoir, the French traveler Ernest Devergier de Hauranne bemoans the dramatic changes in American public speech, which he claims has become "even more vulgar" than the "pack of blood-thirsty wolves" who have taken over the public sphere and listen to it.[5] This arena with its "wild language" and "vulgar" orators became increasingly resistant to women's attempts to contribute to the language that defined it. Friends, family, and academic institutions actively discouraged women who wanted to speak publicly and shunned those who actually dared to address the public from the podium. Lucy Stone, for example, was denied admission to a public speaking class at Oberlin and finally was allowed to audit it only if she agreed to sit quietly. Francis Maria Stewart, another aspiring public speaker, braved the disapproval of her family and fiancé to give four lectures in Boston in 1833, but gave up public speaking because she felt that she "made [her]self contemptible in the eyes of many."[6] Even more contemptible to both male and female members of her 1830s' audiences was Fanny Wright, whose insistence on speaking publicly transformed her, according to Catherine Beecher, into a "great masculine person . . . intolerably offensive and disgusting."[7] Forty years later, Elizabeth Cady Stanton refused to reconsider her conclusion that Victoria Woodhull's famous orations undermined her political usefulness to the woman's suffrage movement. Later still, many scholars of nineteenth-century American oratorical culture have concluded from such unequivocal evidence that the contributions of female orators were negligible.[8]

The persisting tendency to equate nineteenth-century political life with men's, rather than women's, public speech[9] and to underestimate the role of the female voice in public discourse constitutes the point of departure for my project. In the book that follows I show that discourses about the female voice – its sound, tone, and volume, for example – play a central role in the attempts of commentators to define and enforce the social changes instituted by the emerging bourgeoisie, and thus that the female voice assumed a public function, despite theories that argued women inherently lacked the capacity for public activity. In so doing, I show that the female voice became a subject, in both oral and written debate, around which ideas about and challenges to the new middle class revolved and were temporarily resolved.[10] As the contemporary political theorist Jürgen Habermas has shown, the kinds of interchange I examine play vital roles in the public life of any society. Less a physical than a conceptual entity, the public sphere is created, Habermas argues, whenever and wherever a nation's citizens assemble to discuss political issues.[11] Public language, like the sphere that it produces, is fluid, diffuse, and hard to locate – it is produced by official verbal exchange, but also, as scholars have illustrated, by diverse forms of written communication.[12] And, as I will show, debate about the female voice and its contribution to the creation of a distinctly American identity[13] occurred in all of these forms – writing, oratory, and conversation – throughout the nineteenth century. I focus not on the few women who actually spoke in public, but on the vital role that discussions about the voices of American women played in negotiating social change. In the process, I aim to expand our understanding of both the nation at a crucial moment in its evolution and the public power of the women within it.

Scholars of nineteenth-century American culture have recently explored the feminist implications of Habermas's model of public language for gendered notions of the separate spheres.[14] Nina Baym, Cathy Davidson, Lori Ginzberg, and Christine Krueger, among others, have illustrated that the diverse kinds of historical, moral reform, and religious writing that American women produced contributed to the discussions ongoing within and constituting the public arena.[15] Women's fiction, as Nina Baym, Cathy Davidson, Mary Kelley, and Jane Tompkins have shown, made powerful contributions to nineteenth-century public debate as well.[16]

However, there are several advantages to focusing specifically on the female voice and the cultural significance that accrues to it. First of all, such attention reveals the profound influence that the female voice exerted on the various forms of speech that shaped the public arena. As scholars have illustrated, some woman-authored novels, including *Uncle Tom's Cabin,* reinforced middle-class sociopolitical ideals, even as they exerted immense political influence on their audiences. But other novels focused on the female voice and its

4

cultural role, and in so doing, I argue, they pose an even more profound challenge to the distinction between public and private spheres. Thus, when women authors include the female voice in their narratives, they intervene in public discourse even more radically than scholars have imagined. Indeed, as I illustrate in the following chapters, many writers, both male and female, highlight the female voice in their narratives in order to lend rhetorical weight to the political import of their texts. Such invocations indicate that great political significance was attached to the female voice throughout the nineteenth century. Other writers explore the relevance of the female voice to narrative in greater detail, focusing on the female voice not only to enforce their political message but to determine the extent to which the novel can appropriate the political power of that voice. By placing the female voice at the center of their texts, these novelists attempt to overcome what Claire Kahane has identified as the inevitable representation in writing of the speaking voice's absence.[17] The numerous politically persuasive female voices that surface in novels represent, I argue, the hope of writers that novels can influence political debate and finally transform middle-class culture. And so because these fictional voices represent novelists' attempts to deploy within narrative the political power of the female voice – in short, to bridge the gap between "real" and representational worlds – they become a particularly rich place to search for traces of that voice's cultural significance.

While attention to the female voice reveals its centrality to a wide range of public discourses, finally such an analysis enables us to see why, despite the expectations of many writers and significant scholarly evidence to the contrary, the nineteenth-century public sphere continues to be associated with male privilege.[18] In her summary of the current status of gender in Victorian America, Linda Kerber comments on this persistent identification and concludes that even "after we grant that women are not marginal, we are left with an inherited narrative that treats them as outsiders."[19] This inherited narrative, I argue, has succeeded in perpetuating the notion, in the face of increasing conflicting evidence, that women are "naturally" outsiders because one of its primary rhetorical devices – the female voice – has remained unanalyzed. Coexisting with recent reevaluations of the public nature of women's speech and writing, these unassessed accounts of the female voice have inadvertently limited their revisionist power. Thus, analyzing the female voice's role in the written and verbal discourse that constitutes public culture enriches existing narratives of both nineteenth-century life and women's contributions to it.

The time span of this project – roughly the 1830s through the 1880s – is determined by my interest in the emergence, consolidation, and contestation of nineteenth-century middle-class consciousness. While I highlight the historical context of the periods treated in the study, my attention remains focused throughout upon a particular vehicle through which patriarchal culture operates – arguably, in other periods and countries but for the purposes of this study in nineteenth-century America – to protect and perpetuate its power in the face of social change. Because the novel has so often been identified by scholars as both a reflector and disseminator of middle-class ideology,[20] I turn to it in order to analyze the role of the female voice in the evolution of bourgeois ideals. I assess a wide range of canonical and noncanonical novels by writers who use a theme that pervades nonfiction prose so that they can enter into particular political debates. Thus, both in their content and in their diverse relations to the literary canon, these novels consistently erase subsequent distinctions between literature and social history.[21] In order to locate these texts in the cultural atmosphere that motivated their writing, I begin each chapter with an overview of the specific political conversation to which each novel contributes by using the female voice. I treat the novels to which I then turn as textually dense cultural documents that respond to and so extend the political discussions that engage them.[22] By re-creating as much as possible the fluidity that characterized relations between these nineteenth-century "literary" and "historical" texts, I hope to move beyond the ideological conventions that now tend to define each discursive form so that I can assess a system of power that permeates

6

both nonliterary and literary texts, and that is disseminated effectively through a complex interplay between the two genres.

More specifically, I begin the project by showing that the separation of women's speech from the public arena, rather than being either inevitable or total, was a process that depended on the attention that men paid to the sound of women's talk and more particularly to the desires that sound produced. In short, I establish a clear relation between the creation and reinforcement of the nineteenth-century public sphere and the depictions of women's voices that occur repeatedly in American fictional and historical texts. By examining, within the context of contemporary accounts of women's speech, one novel from the 1830s and one from the 1880s that directly address the influence of the female voice on women's ability to engage in public life – Sarah J. Hale's *The Lectures* (1839) and Henry James's *The Bostonians* (1886) – I am able to analyze the particular strategies by which rapt male listeners interpret women's eloquent and politically charged talk in order to reinforce the "natural" gender differences they assume to be innate in women's speech. By tracing the process through which men's attention to women's voices both marginalizes women from public life and consolidates the masculinity of an emerging political arena, I make visible the special interests at work within, and furthered by, literary figurations of women's speech. Yet I show that, far from being inevitable, the separation of women both from public life and from the speech that shapes it is a process enacted and reenacted within the pages of American writing for the purpose of reinforcing the masculinity of the newly reconfigured public sphere. And so I also suggest that precisely because women's public liminality is a process, it lends itself to intervention and even to reversal.

I then illustrate the socially disruptive potential of women's public speech by analyzing the critique mounted by a minority of literary and linguistic thinkers of the 1850s, first, against the separation of the public and private spheres that came to dominate American culture and, second, against the role that the female voice played in shaping them. Contributing to this reanalysis are Herman Melville's

7

Pierre (1852) and E. D. E. N. Southworth's *The Fatal Marriage* (1859), for they show how the sexually explicit subject matter, rather than the eroticized sound, of women's voices recenters their speech in the public sphere from which it has been displaced and, in so doing, I argue, complicate and even temporarily destabilize the imaginative apparatus by which nineteenth-century bourgeois culture defined and recognized itself. In both texts, women's voices, as Homi Bhabha has noted, operate as "counter-narratives of the nation that continually evoke and erase its totalizing boundaries – both actual and conceptual" and thereby "disturb those ideological manoeuvres through which imagined communities are given essentialist identities."[23] In short, I show, first, that by midcentury a minority of American writers and thinkers had begun presenting women's sexually specific articulations as direct, complicating interventions in the nation's understanding of one of its crucial ideological constructions; and, second, that their reconceptualization constitutes an important departure point for reconsidering the impact of the female voice and the speech it enables on nineteenth-century American political life.

While the first two chapters of this project provide a revisionist account of how women's voices influenced the nation's understanding of its public activity, the four final chapters provide examples of the specific political contributions that a diverse group of women writers made by embedding as a central theme in their politically motivated fictions the complex relation between the female voice and women's public speech. In Chapters 3 through 6 I show how their depictions of the female voice and the public speech it generates reinforce women writers' contributions to a wide range of political movements in the nineteenth century. For example, I show how, within the nativist movement that flourished in the 1830s, Maria Monk's tract, *The Awful Disclosures* (1836), explores the usefulness of emerging discourses about the female voice for political writing by presenting the sexual abuse that nuns experience within convents as a series of constraints and assaults on their voices. The narrative voice that "breaks silence" in order to tell its story of sexual abuse replicates outside the convent walls the disobedient, subversive voices of the few nuns within the text who resist Catholic oppression by speaking publicly about it. By metonymically linking the narrative voice to the female voices it describes, Monk's text exercised immense political sway over a public that increasingly identified the nation's integrity with the voices of American women and was becoming anxious about the Roman Catholic immigrants who were invading its geopolitical borders and threatening the bodily boundaries of the iconographically figured "American woman."

The chapters that follow continue to explore this evolving association in female-authored narrative between the female voice and women's speech. Turning to the slavery debates that overlapped with and were largely indebted to nativist political activism,[24] I show how the divergent ways that Caroline Lee Hentz and Harriet Jacobs depict women speakers responding to the southern male oratory that enforces sexual as well as racial inequities work to persuade readers of *The Planter's Northern Bride* (1854) and *Incidents in the Life of a Slave Girl* (1861) to accept the writers' different political views. In an analysis of Elizabeth Stuart Phelps's contribution to the women's labor reform movement of the 1870s, I then argue that *The Silent Partner* (1871) details how working women's voices directly reflect their dire work conditions and more specifically the sexual consciousness that those conditions create. By depicting a woman whose career as a public speaker is motivated by these voices and the diverse sexuality they enunciate, Phelps extends existing labor reform rhetoric that consistently invoked bourgeois sexual standards as normative. Finally, I show how the woman's suffrage project of "gaining a voice" depends, in Lillie Devereux Blake's *Fettered for Life* (1874), on the ability of a cross-dressing woman reporter to represent publicly the silenced, shattered voices of the many women whose traditional clothing marks them as inferior to and defenseless against predatory men. In this chapter, as in the three that precede it, I show how the interplay between the female voice and the public speech it promotes or confounds reinforces the political import of female-authored narrative by triggering for the public the significance of women's language.

While careful attention to the female voice's role in public culture reveals a rich tradition of women's writing that gains political power by playing upon the terms of women's exclusion from public life, such an analysis also provides a historical context in which to place subsequent accounts of gender, sexuality, and language. As Camille Roman has stated, the question of how or if language is "comprehended and used differently by women and men" in the United States has "consistently recurred in the fields of psychoanalysis, anthropology, linguistics, and literary criticism and theory since the turn of the century."[25] The following pages provide a larger historical continuum in which to place and to reconsider the language debates that have absorbed so much critical attention in the twentieth century. From the context I establish, we can see, for example, that the complex, compelling relationship between language and sexuality, forged by Freudian and more particularly Lacanian psychoanalytic thought, extends into the twentieth-century paradigms that have been rooted in American thought since the early nineteenth century. Jacqueline Rose points out that "the force of psychoanalysis is . . . precisely that it gives an account of patriarchal culture as a transhistorical and cross-cultural force."[26] As I show, it is precisely because the interplay between sexuality and language that underpins psychoanalytic theory worked in nineteenth-century America to construct and then complicate the separate spheres within the nation's social, political, and cultural structures that psychoanalysis was able so quickly and persistently to resonate in American thought.

Recent anthropological, psychological, and empirical linguistic studies continue to show the force of nineteenth-century figurations of women's speech. Methodologically diverse scholars concur that in the United States "gender-based differences in language are fairly minimal in language structure, but pervasive in language use."[27] This has led many social commentators to produce a "two-cultures" view of Americans' speech that oddly echoes the ideology of separate spheres. As summarized by proponent Deborah Tannen, the two-culture theory holds that "boys and girls grow up in different worlds . . . and as adults they travel in different worlds" that inculcate and then reinforce "different expectations about the role of talk."[28] Calling for an interdisciplinary practice that would overcome the limitations of any single methodology, feminist linguistic theorists have recently encouraged studies of language and gender that explore how " 'women' and 'men' are constructed as social categories."[29] Thus, by providing, in the following chapters, an assessment of that process in nineteenth-century America, my work creates a framework for understanding how and why such categories persist in the twentieth century.

1

Bawdy Talk

The Politics of Women's Public Speech
in Henry James's *The Bostonians*
and Sarah J. Hale's *The Lecturess*

In an 1813 letter to grammarian John Waldo, Thomas Jefferson wrote that in the United States "the new circumstances under which we are placed, call for new words, new phrases, and for the transfer of old words to new objects."[1] Jefferson's comment has come to epitomize, for scholars of American linguistic and political reform, the links between the two. As Cynthia Jordan notes, antebellum "authors' views on language were tied in with their views on sociopolitical leadership."[2] Kenneth Cmiel likewise traces in public speakers' move from "aristocratic" to middling, or "common," rhetoric the changing political atmosphere of mid-nineteenth-century America.[3]

Central to political reform projects throughout the nineteenth century was the assertion, among both linguists and politicians, that politics and public language were unequivocally male prerogatives. The abiding links between masculinity, public language, and political influence were forged, according to Jordan, at the earliest moment of American national identity and resolved one of the first problems facing the nation's statesmen: "The problem confronting the founding generation . . . was how to devise a system of sociopolitical leadership capable of securing popular acceptance, and the solution they envisioned was the creation and maintenance of a male educated elite that could use language as a means of social and psychological control" (18). Though this model never held uncontested sway over American audiences, by the nineteenth century escalating challenges to these elite men's authority compelled them, as Cmiel notes, to modify their rhetorical practices dramatically, identifying increasingly with their audience rather than preaching to it, in order to maintain their control. Yet if the tone of male elite speakers became more conciliatory and less erudite in attempts to simulate their audience's education level and consciousness, the content of their speech relied more on images of manhood, often, as in Lyman Beecher's speeches, invoking the explicitly classed and gendered image of "the common man" and the political conflicts facing him in order to evoke audience response.

Women began attempting to intervene in this historically male arena of U.S. politics in the 1830s. Yet, as numerous scholars have pointed out, women's limited involvement in public life initially depended upon the "physical weakness, sentimentality, purity, meekness, [and] piousness" that defined their femininity.[4] Rather than calling into question the gender identifications of public and private spaces, women's political activism relied on the power accruing to domesticity and so failed to challenge overtly the masculinity of the nineteenth-century political arena. Nevertheless, as "the right of women to influence politics by speaking from the public platform became a heated issue," those who dominated the political arena began to develop strategies to ensure that the public sphere remained an exclusively and "naturally" masculine domain.[5]

The masculinity of American political culture was subsequently consolidated by political processes that continually reenacted the exclusion of women.[6] As Baker notes, "The notion of womanhood served as a sort of negative referent that united all white men. It . . . made gender, rather than other social or economic distinctions, the most salient political division. Men could see past other differences and find common ground with other men" (630). Election locations reinforced the increasing homosociality of nineteenth-century politics. Occurring in saloons, pubs, and other public male meeting places, political elections, as well as political rhetoric, identified and prescribed dominant forms of manhood.

By defining the characteristics of "male" language as distinct from women's speech, language reformers, as well as politicians, attempted to enforce the strict masculinity of nineteenth-century politics. Yet they accomplished this not so much by creating theories of men's language as by producing a linguistic discourse on women's speech. In highlighting the tone of the female voice, as opposed to its content, and in linking that tone to the female body, linguists tried to place woman's speech firmly in the private arena. Claiming to have discovered a "natural," socially unconstructed link between the female voice and body, linguists strategically policed women's vocal intervention in political culture. The enduring effectiveness of their strategy is evidenced by current critical accounts of women's public speech in nineteenth-century America, which consistently fail to acknowledge the political interests structuring the associations between women's speech and sexual identity.[7]

Within this context of linguistic theories of women's language and their impact on women's public speech, I will focus in this chapter on the anomalous figure of the woman political orator as she is imagined in the two nineteenth-century literary texts that take women's speech making most centrally as their subject: Sarah J. Hale's *The Lecturess, or Woman's Sphere* (1839) and Henry James's *The Bostonians* (1886).[8] Though the two texts focus on women speakers during distinct phases of the nineteenth-century suffrage movement, both emphasize the public's response to them, which depends less on the speakers' specific politics than on the political implications of their physical intrusion into a supposedly male arena. By depicting listeners whose reactions to women's public speech replicate those of linguists, Hale and James critique the prevailing assessments of women's relation to language. *The Bostonians* and *The Lecturess* show linguistic theories for what they are: rhetorical strategies masquerading as "essential truths" in order to marginalize women from the political sphere. Yet Hale and James focus on listeners who interpret the woman orator's speech in terms of her body, and they do so not only to highlight the strategy by which male audience members attempt to consolidate the masculinity of the public arena, but also to point out the limits of that strategy by revealing the ways in which the public male identity that so adamantly defines itself in opposition to women's public speech in

14

fact tacitly constructs itself around the speaking woman's body. In delineating the underpinnings of the publicly constituted identities of the men who listen to the women speakers, both texts problematize the masculinity that defined politics and public language in the nineteenth century. Arguing that the feminine inevitably lurks beneath that masculinity, I show how women's "disorderly" speech helps to construct and sustain the supposedly natural and therefore unalterable maleness of the public arena.

"Twanging," "Whiffling," and "Whining": Women's Language

The preeminent linguist Otto Jesperson summarized and gave "scientific" credence to the long-held view that "woman's language" was incapable of accommodating factual information and thus was essentially tonal when, in 1924, he claimed that women's speech was characterized by parataxis. Parataxis, the joining of clauses through coordination rather than subordination, refuses the prioritization of information because it fails to distinguish the relative significance of associated ideas. Jesperson claimed that women primarily use "and," "or," and "but" to link ideas, while "male" clause joining, in structurally distinguishing more important facts from lesser points, is inherently more capable of accommodating and sorting information. According to Jesperson, "The linguistic . . . peculiarity of feminine psychology" renders women incapable of marking hierarchy within the grammatical structure of their language, and so they must do so "emotionally, by stress and intonation, and in writing by underlining," in short, by the tone of their voices.[9] Their "violent changes in intonation" make women less innovative speakers of English, which Jesperson characterizes as "methodical, energetic, business-like and sober."[10] Indeed, it is the "vigour and vividness" of English, in stark opposition to "languid and insipid . . . women's expressions" (*Language*, 247), that make English "expressly *masculine*, . . . the language of a grown-up man [with] very little . . . feminine about it" (*Growth*, 2).

With resounding unanimity, theorists of American English likewise defined women's speech as essentially tonal in order both to determine and to delimit the impact of women's speech on the creation of a distinctly American elocution. Beginning with his 1783 *Grammatical Institute,* Noah Webster argues that, because "the business of Americans [is] ... to promote virtue and patriotism ... [and] to diffuse an uniformity and purity of language,"[11] "young ladies should be taught to speak ... with purity and elegance."[12] While Webster asserts that the "little misses" of the United States are "sweet little beings, with voices az [*sic*] melodious az [*sic*] the notes of the nightingale," he cautions adult women to "let the prime excellence of your karacters [*sic*] be discovered in all your words" (*Collection,* 406–8). Forty years later, in *Notions of the Americans,* Fenimore Cooper asserts that "we speak our language, as a nation, better than any other people speak their language"[13] because the "voices of the American females are particularly soft and silvery" (175). Arguing that "the language, a harsh one at the best, is made softer by our women, especially of the middle and southern states," Cooper specifies the beneficial effects of women's vocal tone on American English (175). In his 1881 "Women and the Alphabet: Ought Women to Learn It?" Thomas Higginson argues that, if women speak publicly, their articulations should draw attention exclusively to the aesthetic quality of their voices: it "is proper for [women] to sing, but indelicate [for them] to speak in public."[14] William Dean Howells likewise finds in women's singing a vocal ideal when, in his 1906 article for *Harper's Bazar* entitled "Our Daily Speech," he asserts that the American woman "must speak as she sang."[15] Reflecting that "the American woman" of the nineteenth century "without doubt ... had the sweetest voice in the world," Howells subsequently claims that it is her "duty" to "trill sweetly as hermit-brushes, or murmur softly as doves," in short "to speak beautifully" (930–3). He thus summarizes more than a century of linguists' thoughts on the significance of the vocal tone, rather than content, of American women's speech.

Linguists, emphasizing the link between women's vocal tone and body, often conceptualize America as one of the tonally pleasing women who supposedly populate the country. Webster claims that

16

for an iconographic "America in her infancy to adopt the present [rhetorical] maxims of the old world, would be to stamp the wrinkles of decrepit age upon the bloom of youth and to plant the seeds of decay in a vigorous constitution" (*Grammatical*, 14). Almost a hundred years later Richard Grant White, in *Words and Their Uses*, similarly equates vocal tone or "style" with "the blush of a blooming beauty."[16] Claiming that "without dinner, [there is] no bloom; [and] without grammar, no style," White goes on to specify the metonymic link between style and the female body. Style, or tone, bearing "no relation whatever to the soundness or the value of the thought which it embodies," is, like its women users, "mere clearness of outline, beauty of form and expression" (64).

Nevertheless, as women's interest in politics increased, linguists correspondingly argued that their vocal tone was deteriorating. Richard Grant White, in his 1881 *Every-Day English,* claims that, while American women are physically attractive, when they open their mouths, they produce "a mean, thin, nasal, rasping tone, by which you are at once disenchanted."[17] According to William Dean Howells, women's speech is not adequately feminine, because its users, in focusing too much on "brilliant" content and on unwomanly expression, sacrifice sound. The woman speaker, according to Howells in his *Harper's Bazar* article, "sometimes spoke through her nose, she twanged, she whiffled, she snuffled, she whined, she whinnied the brilliant things which she was always incontestably saying" (930). In his 1906 article in *Harper's Bazar,* entitled "The Speech of American Women," Henry James describes American English as threatened by the tonal deterioration of its female population as they claim political equality with men. James links women's focus on the content rather than the sound of their voices with their burgeoning interest in the public sphere, when he writes that "the voice of the American woman, enjoying immense exercise, is lifted in many causes, but the last it anywhere pleads is that of its own casual interest or charm."[18] James records a conversation with a young, politically active woman who resents his suggestion that "the vocal sounds with which a woman affects the ear of man may almost at any time save her situation" (38):

> Intelligibly expressed, my young lady's attitude was that discrim-
> inated sounds . . . were at the best such a vocal burden that any
> multiplication of them was to be viewed with disfavor: I had
> indeed to express this *for* her, but she grunted (her grunt
> had, clearly, always passed for charming) an acceptance of
> my formula. . . . Syllables and consonants . . . might be almost
> unlimitedly sacrificed without absolute ruin to a rough sense.
> (47)

This disregard for, even aversion to, their vocal tone is, according to James, a prerequisite of feminist politics, and so, "since the emanci-pation of the American woman would thereby be attested, the . . . sound" of women's speech is sacrificed (48).

Linguists warn that the cacophonous speech resulting from wom-en's interest in politics poses a direct threat to the future of the nation. When safely ensconced in the private arena of the home and more particularly the nursery, women's language reinculcates, by example and ideological articulation, the gendered notions of speech that are needed to maintain a coherent, cohesive, and male political rhetoric. Yet its most eloquent practitioners, as women's political activity increases, expend an impressive amount of their vocal energy bemoaning the general dissipation to which vocally uncooperative American women subject the nation. As early as 1724 Thomas Wilson, in *The Many Advantages of a Good Language to Any Nation,* warns that, because it is increasingly characterized by "Silli-ness," the speech of women threatens national cohesion.[19] Because "the forming of the Tongue . . . and Pronunciation of Children, are the Works of Mothers," Wilson argues that "we shall never improve our Nation to any great purpose, till we make our Language easy" for women to understand and therefore inculcate (38). More than a hundred years later James Fenimore Cooper, in *The American Democrat,* reiterates Wilson's point, commenting that "contrary to the general law in such matters, the women of the country have a less agreeable utterance than the men, a defect that great care should be taken to remedy, as the nursery is the birthplace of so many of our habits."[20] In his 1906 article, William Dean Howells holds the cacophonous utterings of American women responsible for the general dissipation of men's language, claiming that men's speech will not improve "because nothing good is to be expected of them until their mothers and wives reform" (931). James likewise warns, in his 1906 article, that the United States, in putting up with the unruly speech of its women, is flirting with social chaos and that "the word, stripped for action ... [will] become an inexpensive generalized mumble or jumble, a tongueless slobber or snarl or whine, which every one else would be free, and but too glad, to answer in kind," the end result being a completely dehumanized American English sounding like "the moo of the cow, the bray of the ass, and the bark of the dog" (48–9). In an attempt to avert the general contamination that a deteriorated and bestial woman's language threatens, James appeals directly to his listeners: " 'Don't let us have women like that ... in the names of our homes, our children, our national honor, don't let us have women like that!' " (49). The link that linguists create between women's correct tonal enunciation and "our national honor" allows them strategically to rework their figuration of woman's language as dissociated from content-oriented public speech. In arguing that the tone that defines women's speech is essential to the public and national welfare, linguists and men of letters identify a public function for women's speech that reiterates its gendered difference. In so doing they consolidate and perpetuate patriarchal notions of language and gender.

Such writers describe and attempt to curb women's persistent public outspokenness by invoking the female body as an emblem of women's vocal disorder. For them, the female body is both a symbol of woman's language (and all that is problematic about it) and a vehicle for enforcing women's conformity to that feminine language. Noah Webster makes the link between women's vocal and sexual disorderliness explicit by asserting that "the moment a woman suffers to fall from her tung [*sic*] any expressions that indicate the least indelicacy of mind ... she is no longer respected" (*Collection*, 408). Specifying the kinds of vocal transgressions that lead to accusations of impurity, he notes that "when a woman ... suffers double entendres, indecent hints and conversation to flow from her lips in mixed companies, she remooves [*sic*] the barriers of her reputation" (409). In her 1801 text, *The Accidence: Or, First Rudiments of English Grammar, Designed for the Use of Young Ladies,* Ellin Devis likewise claims that for women verbal forwardness leads to charges of sexual forwardness and that "a multitude of words, is no advantage to ... women."[21] With increasing frequency nineteenth-century linguists and social philosophers invoked the precarious sexuality of the speaking female body in order to control women's public utterances. Yet if commentators on women's language attempt to explain women's "aberrative" speech by equating it with the sexual proclivities of their bodies, the frequency with which linguists do so reveals the extent to which their exertions are necessary in order to inculcate women's supposedly "natural" language.

Epitomizing the maneuvers of a wide array of nineteenth-century writers, James figures the disorderliness of the American vocal tone as a woman when he compares it with the European tone. James imagines the American tone to be an "unfriended heroine" and argues that, "whereas the great idioms of Europe ... have grown up at home and in the family, the ancestral circle (with their migrations all comfortably prehistoric), our transported maiden, our unrescued Andromeda ... was ... disjoined from all the associations that had helped to form her manners, and her voice."[22] Having tied the supposed vicissitudes of women's speech to their bodies, James describes how both speech and body lose value for the men who control and rely upon them:

> We have simply handed over our property – not exactly bound hand and foot, I admit, like Andromeda awaiting her Perseus, but at least distracted, *dishevelled, despoiled,* divested of that beautiful and becoming drapery of native atmosphere and circumstance which had, from far back, made, on its behalf, for practical protection, for a due tenderness of interest. (28, emphasis added)

Because the American tone has deteriorated, the woman who is both its symbol and primary user is, according to James, sexually as well as linguistically compromised. She finds herself in this situation, furthermore, as a result of her insensitivity to and her challenging of social norms. Unlike their European sisters, American women exist without proper fear, the key to tonally pleasing woman's language. In Europe, according to James, it is an

> unwritten law that a lady shall speak as a lady . . . she affronts this sensibility at her peril; so that here immediately . . . she finds something to be afraid of . . . she is really perhaps more afraid of it than of anything else in the world; and if that degree of dread . . . strike us as . . . disproportionate, we yet note on occasion that it often accompanies . . . high civility, true urbanity, of the feminine type . . . and it guarantees such felicities. ("Speech of American Women," 35)

If American language is to improve, women must first learn again "all those attitudes of fear that [have] been immemorially considered, in 'Europe,' to grace the feminine character" (34). And women's bodies serve as the vehicles through which fear and thus refined tone are instilled. Once again metonymically linking female language to the body, James criticizes vocally dissenting young women by claiming that they are "all articulating as from sore mouths, all mumbling, whining, and vocally limping and shuffling" (47). As this strategic invocation of the female body suggests, commentators on American English historically have attempted to ensure the exclusive tonality of women's speech by emphasizing the sexual risks that accompany every female attempt to develop a more openly content-oriented speech.

These nineteenth-century accounts of the tone of women's speech not only remained unchallenged but also were often reinforced by subsequent Freudian, Lacanian, and feminist psychoanalytic formulations of the female voice's exclusively tonal role in the psychic and linguistic development of the modern subject. In his 1905 case study of hysteria, Freud repeats linguists' strategic invocations of the female body by dismissing his patient Dora's account of how her sexual mistreatment has led to her tonal aberration so that he might link her vocal malfunction to her frustrated sexual desires.[23] If Freud's account of Dora's tone reiterates linguists' links between women's speech and sexuality, Lacan's description of language acquisition bears an uncanny resemblance to Jesperson's account of strictly gendered speech roles. Associating women's language with the emotive, "nonsensical" sounds that define mother–child communication, Lacan locates women's speech firmly in the nursery and poses it against an essentially virile, phallic, and content-oriented language wielded by the father. While the subsequent efforts of French feminists such as Julia Kristeva and Luce Irigaray have diversified psychoanalytic constructions of the female voice, their work has not challenged its basic linguistic assertion that women's speech is essentially tonal.[24]

My summary of the historical treatment of women's speech suggests an extensive narrative that testifies to the monopoly that male language and its linguistic theorizers have over vocal content. Yet, as I noted earlier, these articulations, though they masquerade as the norm, are not the exertions of a system that is inherent and total, but are its attempts to maintain the illusion of its complete power. While the alignment of tone, rather than content, with women's speech has consistently justified women's relegation to the private sphere, some feminist linguists have recently begun to reevaluate the ruling assumption that content is an essentially male linguistic characteristic and to reconsider the importance of vocal content for women's speech. Deborah Cameron, for instance, has argued that twentieth-century linguistic theories, both structural and semiotic, have fallaciously assumed that content, what Lacan terms the symbolic, is patriarchal.[25] Cameron's analysis has provided a critical point of departure for reanalyses of women's relationship to language and subsequently to the public sphere.[26] While the ensuing readings of *The Bostonians* and *The Lecturess* take part in a current feminist commitment to discerning the extent to which enduring notions about gender and language are culturally constructed, rather than innate and natural, as linguists have historically argued, I will argue that both texts in turn critique, even though they eventually capitulate to, the essentialism of nineteenth-century linguistic models of women's speech. Thus, I will show that, once placed in the context of contemporary accounts of women's speech, James's and Hale's fictional models of the public world that the woman speaker enters highlight the maneuvers, always dependent upon the speaker's body and vocal tone, by which heterosexist manhood came to be equated with and consolidated within the public arena so thoroughly that the language spoken there continues to be considered inherently male.[27]

Boston Lecturesses: Singing Bad Music

Like *The Bostonians, The Lecturess, or Woman's Sphere* tracks the career of a young woman orator who becomes attracted to and finally falls in love with a male audience member adamantly opposed to her public speech. After a lecture that she gives both to support her mother and to prove women's equality, Marian Gayland meets William Farrinder. Though she rejects his first marriage proposal because he insists she give up her career, public humiliation and illness while she is on a public speaking tour in the South convince her to accept William's second offer. Marian's desire to continue her career strains her marriage and finally estranges William, who realizes he has been unforgiving only after Marian dies alone and penniless. While *The Lecturess* depicts in detail what *The Bostonians* hints at – the disastrous effect of marriage and the silence it enforces on women public speakers – both texts explore the process through which promising, powerful women public speakers are initially silenced by heterosexual relations.

The heroines of *The Lecturess* and *The Bostonians* are both Boston lecturesses who personally confront, in a male listener, the sexual oppression that forms the subject of their public speeches. That confrontation, enmeshed in a love plot for both Marian Gayland in *The Lecturess* and Verena Tarrant in *The Bostonians,* is sustained by the male suitors, who, in ignoring the woman's discourse that theorizes their sexual politics, finally silence the woman speaker's critique. Yet if William Farrinder's and Basil Ransom's desires demand the privatization of women's language along with the privatization of their bodies, it also ensures a faltering male identity a secure place within the public arena and political culture that both men so actively police but to which they feel marginal.

Both texts begin by describing men in private spaces that suggest their marginalization. In *The Lecturess* William is reading in his own study, while in *The Bostonians* Basil is reading in his cousin Olive's parlor. Embedded in the intense interiority that the minute description of his room suggests he has painstakingly constructed, William reads about public lecturesses and remarks to himself that it is "time for men to turn hermits, when women become preachers" (4). Although William justifies his seclusion by appealing to the unruliness of women's speech, he is an atypical man according to his cousin George. You "shut yourself up here, in your study," he tells William, "till you forget all that is going on in the world about you. You have no idea of the rapid march of improvement; and there is no reason, that I know of, why woman should not partake of its advantages" (6). If men who are out in the world understand its operations and the changing role that women play in them, those men who remain inside the home and outside normative male culture lose touch not only with women but with other men as well. In fact, it is to "get William out of the house" that George convinces him to attend Marian's public lecture. He uses the female mouth, rather than the words that issue from it, to seduce William into attendance by saying, "Come with me to hear Miss Gayland assert her rights, and then tell me, if arguments uttered by coral lips have not double the influence of those which issue from lips that boast a beard" (7).

William's study, the product and sign of his wealth and leisure, is precisely what Basil desires but feels unable to acquire because of his position as a marginalized southerner. Olive's parlor is a new kind of interior for Basil, who "had never felt himself in the presence of so much organized privacy or of so many objects that spoke of habits and tastes" (45). He is jealous of the privilege that such an interior connotes and, as Judith Fetterley states, is "galled by the sight of women enjoying what he does not have."[28] After numerous professional setbacks, Basil, under the influence of Mrs. Luna's parlor this time, considers asking her to marry him in order to

24

establish himself permanently in such an interior. He imagines himself "in that very chair, in the evenings of the future, reading some indispensable book in the still lamp-light" (206). Basil is "saved" (216) from being economically kept and feminized by Mrs. Luna by a chance conversation about the public lecturess Verena. His mental image of Verena serves Basil as a timely reminder of the power accruing to him because of his masculinity. As Lynn Wardley writes, Basil, "when faced with actual social fusion . . . seeks to resurrect a democratic body governed by visible distinctions," but, in order to do so, "he must recover sexual difference."[29] If he cannot hold his own against the more affluent and better-educated Boston women around him, Basil can exert his heterosexual desire in order to assert his power over Verena and thus to dominate the women who listen to her.

If both William and Basil are, in distinct ways, marginal members of the male communities they inhabit, they are their communities' most vociferous advocates of strictly gendered speech codes. While Basil consistently employs the rhetoric of southern chivalry in his discussions with Verena in order to contain the challenge that her public speech poses to his sense of male entitlement, the strength of his position on women's speech breaks through his otherwise seamless veneer of gentility, causing him to claim, with a fair amount of hysteria according to Claire Kahane, that because their "whole generation is womanized; the masculine tone is passing out of the world; it's a feminine, a nervous, hysterical, chattering, canting age, an age of hollow phrases" (327). Reflecting the attitudes of nineteenth-century American linguists like Howells, Basil's commentary on women's speech poses the "hollow phrases" of women orators against a "masculine character" that is subsequently endangered. Fraught with fears of feminine linguistic contagion, Basil's own language evidences his acute sense of the contingency of his masculinity.

In *The Lecturess* William is likewise an unusually adamant opponent of women's public speech. As he tells Marian, "I have a strongly rooted dislike, call it prejudice if you will, against woman's speaking in public" (38). Though William does not explain to Marian why, though otherwise opinionless, he feels so strongly about her public speech, his domestic fantasizing is revealing. In his ideal world, woman is to be "the beloved companion of man, when, tired of the noise and tumult of business, he hastens to his home, rendered happy or unhappy according to his choice of a partner" (39). A wife must unequivocally reside in one arena so that a husband can be unequivocally identified with the other. As one social commentator succinctly states, because "masculine character" derives "not so much from what women do to us, as from what we do to them, man will be manlier, that he has a true womanly wife."[30] Marriage for William, then, is a wish fulfillment in which his masculinity can be once and for all resolved by the "correct" behavior of his spouse. Like the commentaries of social critics then, both men's rhetoric on women's speech reveals the extent to which their masculinity depends upon their ability to control that speech and thus the power relations that latently structure, and can be deployed at will to stabilize, the public sphere.[31]

William and Basil, though they end up listening to lecturesses speak on women's rights, maintain their categorical resistance both to women's public speech and to its ideology of equal rights by constructing their own narratives about the women who are speaking. William, though lured out of his study by the thought of coral lips, does not actually agree to attend Marian's lecture until George tells him that Marian speaks publicly to support her mother. This explanation provides him with a way to neutralize what she says and to reread it as a reassuring example of familial love. As he listens to her lecture on equal rights, a lecture ironically informed by her childhood remembrances of her mother's oppressed life, William becomes "fascinated by her beauty and conversation; he listened with eager attention to the beautiful thoughts and feelings to which she gave utterance, fancying them a transcript of his own" (32). William's act of hearing rewrites the content of Marian's speech to conform to his notion of appropriate and desirable feminine language. Basil commits an equally dramatic act of mishearing. If Marian speaks because of her mother, Verena speaks to please her father. This rationale allows Basil to dismiss what she says: "She didn't mean it, she didn't know what she meant, she had been stuffed with this trash by her father, and she was neither more nor less willing to say it than to say anything else" (85). While listening to Verena, he transforms her into "a touching, ingenuous victim" whose "charm was her own" and whose "fallacies [were] . . . a mere reflection of unlucky circumstance" (251). In short, he reproduces the patronizing oppression that she describes and uses it to marginalize her speech. Thus, both men strategically dismiss the women's offensive speech by replacing it with the appealing speaker.

William and Basil fix on the speaker's superior vocal tone, which they tie to the female body, in order to marginalize the political content that linguists and writers consistently claimed to be "naturally" incompatible with a pleasing, feminine tone. Before William attends Marian's lecture, he imagines her to be "a coarse, masculine-looking woman, uttering her opinions in a harsh, discordant voice" (10). Yet, for William, both her body and vocal tone are so feminine that they overpower the content of her first speech, which is excised from the text and replaced, for both William and the reader, by his response to it: "Much more she said to the same effect. Her language was pure and elegant, her voice full and round, but at the same time sweetly toned" (12). The fullness, roundness, and elegance that describe Marian's voice simultaneously describe the feminine appeal of her body and so authorize William's interest in the "sweetly toned" way in which Marian speaks rather than in the content of her speech.

The content of Verena's speech at Mrs. Birdseye's home is similarly replaced by Basil's reaction to it. That reaction dramatically spotlights the strategy by which male listeners dismiss the political content of women's speech, focusing instead on the vocal tone that, according to Basil, indicates woman's "essential nature." Overwhelmed by the appeal of Verena's "tone [which is] so pure and rich, and yet so young, so natural" (265), Basil reconstitutes the political parameters of her project, claiming that the necessity of her nature was not to make converts to a ridiculous cause, but to emit those charming notes of her voice ... to please every one who came near her, and to be happy that she pleased. ... He contented himself with ... regarding her as a vocalist of exquisite faculty, condemned to sing bad music. How prettily, indeed, she made some of it sound! (85)

The pleasing sound of Verena's voice is reinforced by the pleasing image of her body as she speaks. That convergence further justifies Basil's erasure of the political content of her speech: "The effect was not in what she said, though she said some such pretty things, but in the picture and figure of the half-bedizened damsel ... the visible freshness and purity of the little effort" (84).

By focusing on the links between the woman speaker's tone and body, both Basil and William uncover their burgeoning desire for the speaker. Yet both men's erotic interest, while supposedly produced by a woman's public speech, actually operates as a strategy for containing that speech and thus consolidating the masculinity of the public sphere. William's love for Marian is the direct result of his obsessive attention to the metonymic relation between her body and vocal tone. To William, Marian seems "to become more lovely with every word she uttered; her eyes, those clear, bright eyes, shone through the tears the subject called forth, and her voice, low and tremulous, was like the sweet tones of music of which we sometimes dream" (29). William's compensatory amplification of Marian's feminine desirability escalates as he listens to her arguments for women's emancipation, operating as an effective containment strategy for his rising male anxiety.

As Verena's career becomes increasingly successful, Basil imbues the feminine attributes of her speech with additional power. When after a year, Basil first hears Verena's voice again, he thinks that it "had developed; he had forgotten how beautiful it could be when she raised it to its full capacity" (265). Her matured speech fixes "his attention ... in a way it had not been yet" (266), almost forcing Basil to acknowledge its content. But he ignores Verena's more powerful rhetoric by interpreting her political message in terms of his erotic interest. Although "certain phrases took on a meaning for him" (266), they make him conscious, not of his latent sexism, but of his desire. He subordinates Verena's compelling political rhetoric to his newly discovered love. Listening to Verena speak, he "simply felt her presence, tasted her voice. . . . [H]e found himself rejoicing that she was so weak in argument, . . . it was a proof that . . . she was meant . . . for privacy, for him, for love" (269). Thus, in a self-serving tautological move reminiscent of linguists' invocations of women speakers' sexuality, Basil constructs Verena's desirability as a product of the tone of her voice and simultaneously as the rationale for not hearing its content.

Both William's and Basil's desire for women speakers is, as I have shown, produced by the women's public speaking, yet both men claim that their desire is "naturally" in conflict with the fact that the women speak publicly. This tactic authorizes them to demand that the women accept public silence as a condition for marriage. While Marian and Verena are able to refuse such a condition on strictly ideological grounds, the importance of William and Basil as audience members threatens and finally subverts the women's ability to speak publicly. Though his desire initiates William into public life, causing him to neglect "his books [and] his tastefully fitted-up study" (32), that desire requires that Marian become a private woman. His marriage proposal becomes the first step in William's active campaign against women's public speaking. Marian rejects marriage by refusing to become silent and disabuses William of his misreading of her motives by saying, "I do not, when I appear before the public, merely echo the opinions of others, learned from books. Every word I speak is dictated by my heart. . . . Mr. Farrinder, remember that you are addressing a lecturess – a public defender of the rights of her sex" (35).

If Marian can adeptly turn down William's marriage proposal on ideological grounds, it is only because she does not yet understand how much she has come to depend upon him as a public listener. In her first speech after his proposal, she realizes the extent to which her public speaking has become a private act between herself and William:

> That night an assembled crowd gazed in admiration upon the faultless beauty of the lecturess, and listened to her eloquent appeal in behalf of woman. Loud applause rang through the vaulted hall. The voice of the many expressed pleasure, if not approval; but the sounds were unheeded and scarcely heard by her for whom they were intended. There was in the vast crowd not one being for whose approval she now cared. One form was missing, one whom night after night she had seen there. His place was now occupied by another. She should not hear his voice at the close of her labors. (43)

William's regular presence in her audience, made possible by his rewriting of her motives and mishearing of her lectures, creates a dependence in Marian. She comes to rely on both his physical presence and the pleasing sound of his voice, separated from its sexist rhetoric on women's public speech. His voice both produces her love and epitomizes its absent object when, having rejected him, Marian recognizes that "years may intervene, before the sound of that dear voice shall gladden her ear" (44).

Separated from William, Marian decides to construct a new audience for herself in the South. Her geographic relocation engages her in national politics that infiltrate both the content of her lectures and her audience's reactions to those lectures. Believing Marian to be an abolitionist, her audience becomes hostile: "It was a severe mortification to Marian, when, instead of the shouts of applause which had always attended her appearance, she was met by hissing and revilings" (54). Marian responds to the vocal aggression of the audience by directly addressing abolition, which further antagonizes the audience, and "assailed on every side by threats and menaces, encountering wherever she turned her eyes malignant and angry looks . . . voice after voice joined in the fearful cry" (56), Marian is finally silenced. Though she escapes, she "was herself no longer" (57). The audience's hostile voices cause Marian to reanalyze her voice and then to hear another one during her ensuing illness. The "still, small voice of conscience, unheard or unheeded amid the noisy shouts of popular approval" (57) convinces her that she speaks out of pride rather than conviction. Attacked both from without and from within her own psyche, Marian finally capitulates to the legal silencing that William demands.

Like Marian, Verena responds to and comes to depend upon the voice of her male suitor. Basil's "charming dialect" – the way he "prolong[s] his consonants and swallow[s] his vowels" (36) – fascinates her. "Pervaded by something almost African in its rich, basking tone" (36), Basil's voice sounds not only regionally but by extension racially distinct and therefore exotic to Verena. Basil's unusual "tone" works to dispel Olive's "shyness," but she develops an immediate dislike for "the way" that he speaks because it reminds her of his political affiliation with "the Southern side" (42) during the war. Yet, because Verena remains impressed by his "very graceful" manner of speaking, she consistently overlooks the political import of Basil's words. As she listens to "his deep, sweet, distinct voice, expressing monstrous opinions with exotic cadences and mild, familiar laughs" (322), Verena dismisses, as "exaggerations," his views and ponders instead the abused past life that produced them. As she does so, she replicates the listening strategies that Basil uses to produce desire for her and thereby becomes complicit in the public silencing with which the novel closes. Verena's attraction to Basil thus reveals the pernicious effect that such listening strategies have on women's ability to hear, and so gauge, their political opponents as well as to be heard by them.

Though Verena's attraction to Basil ultimately ensures her acquiescence to his repressive marriage proposal, it also reveals the nature of the intimate, homosocial world that Verena and Olive create as they fashion and refine Verena's public speaking. Initially attracted to Olive because of the "elegant parlour" that provides her with "a regular dream-like place to sit" (119), Verena soon becomes a permanent fixture in it. As the two women sit intimately together in the parlor's "islands of lamplight," they read "a great deal of history . . . with the . . . thought . . . of finding confirmation that their sex had suffered inexpressibly" (186). Olive's "eloquence" as she speaks to Verena about "the exquisite weakness of women," coupled with the "tone of softness and sympathy" that Olive reserves for her "very private life" (152), forms the basis of the women's intimate interactions. Always "passionately clean," once Verena moves in, Olive "elevate[s] daintiness to a religion" and "her interior shine[s] with superfluous friction, with punctuality, [and] with winter roses" (184). Both Olive's changes to the parlor and Verena's vocal "blossoming" among Olive's "soft influences" indicate the fervency of the women's attraction to each other. Yet the talk that denotes their intimacy becomes the dramatic marker of the threat to their relationship posed by Basil's courtship of Verena. "Voluble, fluent, [and] feverish" as she perpetually discusses Basil's suit, Verena turns the speech that Olive has fostered against her, "smother[ing] her in her own phrases" (317). As the speech that signifies their homoerotic bond is pressed into the service of heterosexual desire, the women are able to express their "wild, personal passion" only by holding each other silently in "the low, dim parlour" (400).

While William's absence from Marian's audience leads to her humiliation and silencing, Basil's relentless presence in Verena's audience not only erodes her relationship with Olive but silences the public speech that flourishes because of it. Basil's realization that Verena was "meant for something different – for love, for him" initiates a courtship that consists of attending her lectures in order to impede her ability to speak not only to Olive but finally to the public. His resisting presence does not affect her lecture at Mrs. Burrage's house and may even enhance it, in part because she enjoys attempting conversions. But after listening to Basil talk for a whole afternoon, Verena returns to Olive silenced and shamed. Huddled in a corner, "unwilling to speak," she seems so "crushed and humbled" that Olive sees it as "a kind of shame" (399). Verena is shamed first into private and then into public silence by Basil's persistent and hostile presence. Though Basil buys a ticket to hear the public speech that should launch Verena's career, "he was not one of the audience; he was apart, unique, and had come on business altogether special" (414). This business is to assert forcefully his right to make Verena's speech private. His desire "to speak to her in private" ensures that Verena will henceforth speak only in private. She tells Basil, "I saw you in your place, in the house, when you came. . . . Then I felt too nervous to speak! I could never, never, if you were there . . . if I attempted to speak – with you sitting there – I should make the most *shameful* failure . . . from the moment I knew you were on the other side I couldn't go on. I was paralysed" (428–30, emphasis added). Basil's public presence repeats the shaming of his private presence. Though Verena pleads with Basil to let her "soothe" her hostile audience "with a word," he relentlessly enforces her public silence by telling her to "keep your soothing words for me" (430).

Though *The Bostonians* ends with the public silencing that indicates Verena's acceptance of Basil's marriage proposal, *The Lecturess* explores how men continue to exert power over women by controlling their speech within marriage. Women's speech immediately becomes a contentious issue in Marian and William's marriage, not only because William demands that his wife confine her "talk" to their "own fireside" but because, even within the domestic arena, he cannot tolerate her vocal superiority. As they argue about Marian's desire to attend a public lecture, William realizes that, compared with his wife, who continually turns his "witticism" against him, he is "very stupid." William's attempts to exert his dominance by insisting that Marian "relinquish all communication with lecturesses and their lectures" thus prove futile because of his inferior rhetorical skills. Marian's talk, even in the home, is too powerful to be confined to it, and so she continues to attend public lectures in the capacity of both listener and speaker. Reduced to voicing his disapproval through silence, William demands, even as they finally forgive each other, that they "never speak of what is past" (90). Though "the light song and laugh of hearts at ease echo through their dwelling" (90), once Marian gives up lectures for motherhood, domestic accord depends on her continual acknowledgment of William's vocal superiority. And so Marian curtails her powerful speech, "relating [only] the events of the day and the little boy's witty speeches to Mr. Farrinder" (93). Once the resisting member of Marian's public audience, William is now her sole listener, defining and delimiting the domestic space by determining the speech appropriate to it.

Both *The Bostonians* and *The Lecturess* thus end with women speakers shamed into public silence through marriage. Yet they also end with formerly marginalized, silenced men wielding greater control of public discourse. If William and Basil confront, in the image of the woman public speaker, the limits of their own power, they also use that image to propel themselves into the public arena. Both novels illustrate the strategic maneuvers by which women's speech is continually, and often violently, policed into its "natural" role of private language by its male listeners' amplification of both the vocal tone and sexual desirability of the woman speaker. Both texts also suggest that this impetus to amplify the "feminine" is produced by male listeners' anxiety about their own limited power, not just in relation to patriarchy, but in relation to the successful public speaking of women who seem too comfortably ensconced in its power structure. By observing the ways in which women's public speech is bound up in and filtered through the female body, we can discover a process by which women have been effectively excluded from the political arena, and so we can revise the pervasive notion that the political and public are "naturally" male domains.

2

"Foul-Mouthed Women"

Disembodiment and Public Discourse in Herman Melville's *Pierre* and E. D. E. N. Southworth's *The Fatal Marriage*

In low, sweet, and changefully modulated notes ... [Isabel] breathed the word *mother, mother, mother!* There was profound silence for a time; when suddenly ... the magical untouched guitar responded with a quick spark of melody.

Herman Melville, Pierre (1852)

Suddenly through the room rang a deep, bell-toned, authoritative voice, that commanded – *"Pause!"* ... *"The first-born daughter of Orville Deville is beyond your prayers"* ... spoke the awful voice of the invisible. A thrill of horror ran through the assembly [at] ... the first word of the unseen speaker.

E. D. E. N. Southworth, The Fatal Marriage (1859)

Literary critics have consistently attempted to account for the strangeness of Isabel's language by placing Herman Melville's *Pierre* in the context of "the thrillers of the times" and even more particularly "Mrs. E. D. E. N. Southworth's prolific domestic novels."[1] However, despite their impulse to pair *Pierre* with Southworth's fiction, scholars have not assessed the precise nature of the similarity between the two writers' projects and the possible cultural significance of their unlikely union. The above quotations provide a starting point for such an analysis by revealing that both writers are fascinated with the female voice and more specifically with the unprecedented power that listeners attribute to it because of its indeterminate position outside or beyond the body of the woman speaker. In this chapter I focus on the opportunities that this physically dis-

35

placed or "disembodied" female voice[2] creates for Southworth and Melville to formulate, within the domestic fiction that depends upon and perpetuates middle-class ideology, a radical critique of some of its major premises.[3] Like the women orators' voices discussed in the preceding chapter, these disembodied voices activate their listeners' interest, but their rhetorical power is not limited by the strategies that fictional audiences often use to contain women speakers. Because the absence of the woman speaker's body confounds the mechanism by which intratextual listeners ignore the content of women's speech, this new female voice is able to produce public speech that has a profound, unmitigated impact on its middle-class audience. With its enhanced political effectiveness, this public speech represents, and reinforces the political impact of, the narratives that feature it. However, because both novels draw upon and engage in ongoing debates about the female voice's role in middle-class culture, we can understand the full significance of Southworth's and Melville's alternative accounts of women's language only in the context of contemporary attitudes regarding woman's language and sexuality, and the impact of both on middle-class America.

Though audience attention to the sound of women's speech, as I showed in the preceding chapter, worked to displace many women from public life, theorists of American English throughout the eighteenth and nineteenth centuries consistently assert that the American woman's elocution, because it reflects her irreproachable sexual purity, refines the quality of public debate in which American men engage. Acting as "a young man's best security against . . . a dissipated life,"[4] American women's speech, according to Noah Webster in his 1790 *Collection of Essays and Fugitiv Writings,* prepares men to enter the public sphere and to elevate the rough political language spoken there. Even as they displaced the vast majority of women from public debate, American men throughout the nineteenth century, according to historian Dennis Baron, were "advised to listen to women" because their "language was said to bring polish and civilization to an otherwise rude and barbarous tongue."[5] The "Female's conversation" was able to elevate men's language and by extension the entire nation's speech because, as social commentator John Pintard asserts, it was a direct manifestation of women's own physical as well as mental "pur[ity], chast[ity], and unaffected[ness]."[6]

Convinced by linguists that their speech reflected a sexual purity that elevated the entire nation's utterance, women became fastidious speakers, committed to maintaining the linguistic "uniformity and purity" in which Webster had taken such pride[7] and careful to avoid the "slovenly and uncouth utterance" that William Dean Howells claimed, in his 1906 article, "Our Daily Speech," indicated women's sexual dissipation.[8] The linguistic efforts of American women caused late-nineteenth-century European language theorist Otto Jesperson to remark publicly that the speech of "American and especially Boston ladies" was singularly "prudish."[9] Reporting that these women "invent innocent and euphemistic words" because they "are shy of mentioning certain parts of the human body . . . by the direct . . . denominations,"[10] Jesperson notes with dismay that they speak "of the *limbs* of a piano" (*Growth,* 240) rather than its legs.[11] Yet, despite late-nineteenth-century European linguists' criticism of the extremes to which American women went in order to articulate their sexual virtue and thereby raise the expressional level of the nation, American men of letters continued to concur with Webster's earlier contention that the purity of women's conversation had a major "influence" on "the manners of [the entire] nation" (*Collection,* 28).

Though the vast majority of American linguists enthusiastically endorsed the refined feminine speech that supposedly infused the public sphere and produced a pure, cohesive national utterance, a countermovement of transcendental language theorists in the 1850s became openly critical of bourgeois Americans' increasing linguistic avoidance of the body. By emphasizing the "centrality of female purity" and "impos[ing] limits on public expression of sexuality,"[12] the American middle class rising to prominence in the 1850s, according to Ralph Waldo Emerson, was "corrupting" rather than refining both Americans' subjectivity and their speech.[13] Because of its rejection of the body, the passionless, bourgeois woman's speech so valued by most linguists was destroying the rugged, physical subject matter that, according to transcendental thinkers, characterized American English and the national identity of its users. As the English that middle-class women spoke increasingly failed to reflect in its subject matter the experiences of Americans' bodies, this minority of theorists argued that the vigorous vocal content that once typified the nation's language was also destined to become devoid of bodily experience and sensation. Dramatically breaking with the majority of language commentators, they thus encouraged women to restructure their speech to include physical and sexual experiences.

Using as a starting point this contradictory opinion regarding women's employment of sexually explicit subject matter, I want to explore in the following pages the anomalous figure of the "foul-mouthed" woman speaker as she appears in the two midcentury novels remarkable for and linked because of their interest in the revisionist possibility of the female voice. In both Herman Melville's *Pierre* (1852) and E. D. E. N. Southworth's *The Fatal Marriage* (1859)[14] it is the physical, rather than rhetorical, dissociation of women's voices from their bodies that enables the heroines[15] to circumvent the strategies that contain their speech and thereby to recover command over the sexually specific subject matter that women have surrendered in their attempt to raise the nation's vocal standard. By generating public speech that reveals bourgeois women's covetousness of men's public privilege and the covert sexual practices that, once known, damage men's preeminent position in the public arena, these female voices destabilize the "natural" identification of women with the private sphere and men with the public sphere and the language spoken there. And so, by incorporating and extending in their fictions transcendental theories of women's speech, Southworth and Melville reimagine the role of women's language in American culture and mount a powerful critique of the gender, linguistic, and sexual codes of their middle-class audiences.

Strong Coarse Talk

In his early 1850s commentary on language, compiled in *The Primer of Words,* Walt Whitman describes the effects of a burgeoning middle-class consciousness on Americans' language. Appalled by "the remarkable non-personality and indistinctness of modern . . . talk," Whitman attributes America's linguistic decline to its users' "lack of an avowed, empowered, unabashed . . . sex."[16] He holds responsible "good folks" whose "linguistic prudery" seems to "lingeringly pervade all modern . . . conversation." With their "delicate lady-words . . . [and] gloved gentleman-words," the "castrated persons, impotent persons . . . men not fond of women, [and] women not fond of men," who, according to Whitman, make up the middle class, destroy Americans' "strong, cutting, beautiful rude words" and by extension "the liberty and brawn of these states."[17] America's linguistic deterioration has been brought about not by the sexual licentiousness of its women speakers, as linguists suggest, but by the language's failure to register the full force of sexuality. This failure, according to Whitman, leaves a profound gap between American consciousness and the English that represents it. Because "poets, historians, biographers, and the rest" have capitulated to "the filthy law" that makes "sex, womanhood, maternity, desires, lusty animations, organs, [and] acts . . . unmentionable," these bodily realities are forced "to skulk out of literature with whatever belongs to them" (Whitman to Emerson, 737). Asserting that "this filthy law has to be repealed" (737), Whitman suggests that linguistic "filthiness" results less from the articulation of bodily drives, as the middle class claims, than from the failure of American English to reflect bodily experience.

Whitman finds in the working class, rather than in the middle class, a more physically oriented American English that realigns sexuality and speech and thereby provides a paradigm for American English as a whole. Using his own body to emphasize the physical immediacy of workers' speech, Whitman admits that he loves "to go away from books, and walk amidst the strong coarse talk of men as they give muscle and bone to every word they speak."[18] The muscle that the workingman brings to his job structures his speech as well, creating a more physical language. Though in "polite" company there "have not yet been served up . . . words to be freely used in books, rooms, at table . . . to specifically mean the act male and female" (*Primer,* 745), Whitman finds that "among fighting men, gamblers, thieves, [and] prostitutes" "many of the slang words . . . are powerful words" and argues that "these words ought to be collected – the bad words as well as the good – many of the bad words are fine" (736). Though the middle class's refusal to supply "words" for the actions of sexually healthy bodies results in "putrid cadaverous meaning" (745), the unrestrained, bodily vocabulary that is produced by and reflects physical work provides a healthy linguistic alternative and therefore should make up "the great Dictionary of the future," which must "follow the open voices of the Americans – for no other nation speaks with such organs" (*Other,* 811).

While Whitman advocates using words that are more descriptive of Americans' physical and erotic lives, the tone in which these "limber, lashing-fierce words" are spoken must enhance their content as well. While "all passions" should be "latent . . . in a great user of words" (*Primer,* 742), the orator must carefully balance them both in life and in the speech that reflects it. Because "all sorts of moral . . . deformities are inevitably returned in the voice" (738), Whitman advocates sexual awareness but cautions against sexual excess or "deviance." According to Whitman, "Gluttony" and "brandy" are "generally fatal to the perfection of the voice," while "masturbation [and] inordinate going with women, [also] rot the voice" (737). And so in order to achieve "great vocalism" one must have experience "with woman . . . and experience with man," but remain sexually moderate and therefore "chaste" (737). If successful, the tone or "fibre and charm of the voice" will fully represent the vitality of Americans' bodies by making "words sing, dance, kiss, do the male and female act, [and] bear children" (742). Once Americans combine the body-oriented content of the working people with this erotically infused tone, Whitman is convinced that American English will capture bodily experience and thus that Americans will be "the most perfect word users" and "the most fluent and melodious voiced people" (732).

To that end transcendentalists suggest that all speakers, but especially women, reincorporate a vigorous sexual energy into both the tone and content of their talk. While Emerson argues that all Americans should make use of obscene words normally "excluded from polite conversation,"[19] Whitman targets the women's speech that is responsible for making the body and its sexuality "impolite" topics in the first place. Because "the *words* of Maternity" include not only the diminished vocabulary of the pure, middle-class woman, but "all the words that were ever spoken," Whitman argues that "the mouth of the full-sized mother, daughter, wife, amie, does not offend by using any one" of these "reborn words" (*Primer,* 734). He asserts that women are capable not only of recovering words prohibited by middle-class culture, but of producing new ones that undermine bourgeois ideology as well. Because "an immense number of new words are needed" to describe "the vital equality of women with men . . . politically, socially, and in business" (737), Whitman predicts that women will expand American English to accommodate a new feminine consciousness that challenges middle-class ideology.

Committed to achieving equality between the sexes, writer and public orator Angela Heywood became one such woman by devoting her career to changing the passionless utterances of middle-class women. With transcendental thinkers like "Higginson, Bronson Alcott," "Garrison . . . [and] Emerson" for her "immediate teachers,"[20] Heywood began lecturing publicly in the 1880s as part of a program to implement freer, more sexually explicit rhetorical practices and thereby to enforce sexual equality between the sexes. Heywood was immediately attacked by moralist and politician Anthony Comstock, who claimed that of all the "public meetings [that he attended] where foul-mouthed women"[21] advocated Free Love practices in order to destroy sexual chastity, Angela Heywood's "vile" speech was "the foulest address" he "ever heard."[22] In her response to Comstock, Heywood implements her program to use "true words" to describe sexual functions and organs. Reversing his claim that she is "lost to all shame,"[23] Heywood proclaims that "if Comstock's own penis was well-informed and behaved"[24] he would not object to her "open" and "frank" conversation "about man."[25] Heywood contends that the inequity in men's and women's ability to speak about "the mysteries of Sex, the secrets of coition, [and] the momentous potencies of Love"[26] results from the role that women's pure speech plays in "civilizing" Americans' speech and enables men like Comstock to dominate women sexually and vocally. As long as "the penis is *known about* . . . [but] not *spoken out about*"[27] and women continue to lack "formulas of expression concerning the male generative organ," Heywood argues that there will be "no companionable exchange in dialect"[28] or sexuality. Using as her rhetorical arena public lecture halls and the Free Love publication, *The Word*, a vehicle of communication that specified the idiom in which her sexual revolution was to take place, Heywood claims, as had her predecessor Whitman, that, once "we . . . have true, proper words" ("Personal Attitudes") for human sexuality, society will be transformed.

Though men enforce women's sexual and vocal inequality, Heywood argues that as long as the bourgeois woman continues to believe that her purity is reflected in the bodilessness of her speech, she will continue to be complicit in destroying women's freedom. Pretending "that intelligent expression . . . [of] sex . . . is 'obscene,' 'vulgar,' [and] 'dirty',"[29] " 'refined,' 'learned,' [and] 'delicate' women" not only are masking the real extent of their sexual knowledge but, more important, tacitly "are supporting pillars of social evil" ("Personal Attitudes"). Thus, Heywood claims that the purity and virtue upon which bourgeois women pride themselves are in fact " 'pure' ignorance and idiotic 'virtue' " that make girls unable "to speak of the beauty, fullness, exhilerating [*sic*] and creative value of the Penis" ("Woman's View No. 4"). This vocal inability creates in woman either "an over-charged, vibrating Womb unduly craving the offices of . . . the Penis" (ibid.) or an "acquiescing, dead-level [sexual] servility."[30] Even worse, in men it produces a "lecherous, treacherous irresponsibility" (ibid.) that "manufactures 'prostitutes,' 'harlots,' 'whores,' [and] 'strumpets,' " instead of "glorif[ying] woman."[31] Thus, because the bourgeois woman equates female purity with vocal denial of the body, she inadvertently endorses the sexual victimization of all women.

In their first step toward equality, Heywood contends that women must appropriate existing sexual vocabularies, clearly articulating hitherto taboo words. Appalled by " 'ladies' in parlors who call man's penis his 'teapot' and his 'thing,' "[32] Heywood argues that "if man says 'womb' without rising heat or dishonest purpose . . . woman [should] say 'penis' without blushing squirm or sheepish looks."[33] Arguing that the "penis, its doings and not-doings, its use and responsibility has much need to be . . . talked . . . about," Heywood asks her female audience why they "cringe and blush at [the word] penis?"[34] According to Heywood, "the force of woman's tongue" publicly describing men's "penises [as] over-loaded with white, child-making blood"[35] would go far not only toward asserting vocal equality between the sexes, but toward controlling male sexual activity in private. In saying "penis" publicly, Heywood attempts to bring the politics of the bedroom under public surveillance and so to control what she terms "predatory penis commerce" ("Men, Women, and Things," December 1883).

Heywood argues that, once comfortable articulating words with a sexually explicit content, women and all other speakers should choose words that have a sound more consonant with the male procreative anatomy. Thus, because "man's vigor is not [exactly] expressed by" the word "penis" ("Sexual Nomenclature"), women should consider replacing that term with ones that in sound as well as in content "exactly define sex-organs and their mutual use" ("Penis Literature"). Though her attitude toward sexuality and women's speech diverges from most nineteenth-century linguists', Heywood endorses the prevailing linguistic equation of vocal tone with women's speech[36] when she notes that, because "penis is a smooth, musical, almost feminine word, . . . man is instinctively true to [his] nature in coining the word cock to define [his] creative power" ("Sexual Nomenclature"). In arguing that "cock," because it "sound[s] harsher, should be used instead" of "penis" (ibid.), Heywood, like Whitman, argues that, in both their tone and content, words should reflect the sexual activities they describe.

43

Though this minority of language reformers actively and often successfully encouraged women for more than half a century to incorporate sexuality into the content as well as the tone of their daily speech, twentieth-century language commentators have overlooked the movement's significance in their own historical, psychoanalytic, and structural and semiotic linguistic formulations of women's relation to language. Their attitudes inadvertently shaped by the dominant pre-twentieth-century linguistic assessment of women's speech, these scholars have often reinforced the notion that women's speech avoids socially and sexually seditious subject matter in order to adorn and elevate American English rather than to contribute directly to its political content. Scholars have interpreted contemporary women's residual vocal traditions as a sign, not of the enduring prescriptive power of the earlier model of women's speech, but of its essential accuracy. Therefore, either they have concluded that men "naturally" have greater ability with a broad range of subject matter while women have a greater natural facility with the sound of language, or they have studied the cultural, linguistic, and social effects of such unalterable differences.[37] Because this significant and diverse critical work has not accounted for the cultural and historical origins of pervasive social attitudes toward gender and speech in the United States, it has extended and consolidated the hegemony of dominant nineteenth-century accounts in our current consciousness of gender and language.

Yet by reassessing Melville's and Southworth's fictional depictions of "foul-mouthed" women speakers in the context of transcendental thinkers' alternative accounts of women's speech, I will suggest that we broaden our understanding of women's relation to content-oriented language and the public sphere in which it is spoken, not only in the 1850s but in the late twentieth century. By depicting in their fictions the practical implications of transcendental theories of women's language, Southworth and Melville imagine their impact on the middle-class community. In both novels, the startling physical distance between the voice and body of the woman speaker confounds the listening strategies that, as I showed in the preceding chapter, some male audience members use to ignore the content of women's speech. Because they compel their listeners' complete attention, these female voices are able to produce public speech that, first, points out women's subversive desire for public power and, second, criticizes the male desire that effectively displaces women from the public sphere. These women's voices thereby challenge and finally undermine the separate-sphere ideology that produces and enforces regressive accounts of women's language. Thus, by depicting women as influencing public, highly political debate, Southworth and Melville reimagine the role of the female voice and women's speech in nineteenth-century American culture and alter the persistent sense that public language is an exclusively male prerogative.

Idolatrous Devotion

Like *Pierre*, *The Fatal Marriage* tracks the effect of a young man's maturation on his relationship to his mother and the patrilineage that she protects for him until he reaches his majority. Despite his childhood marriage to an unknown cousin named Adelaide, Orville, while he recovers from a riding injury, seduces and secretly marries an uneducated but beautiful young woman named Lionne at her father's rural retreat. He returns home promising to come back for her but, once there, falls in love with Adelaide. After confronting Adelaide and Orville with her prior claim and hearing Orville declare his preference for Adelaide, Lionne returns to her father's home and fakes death to keep her father from learning of her dishonor and impending motherhood. With Lionne's supposed death, Orville is next to inherit her father's newly reclaimed estate in Scotland and so realizes for the first time that she was a cousin and social equal. Orville and Adelaide sail for Scotland to claim the Deville inheritance, but Lionne follows them, vowing revenge for her own, her unknowing father's, and her dead child's dishonor. Lionne's campaign succeeds because, unseen, she repeatedly throws her voice into the public gatherings at which Orville celebrates his new social position. Thus, while *The Fatal Marriage* depicts what *Pierre* stops short of showing – the disembodied female voice actually

45

engaging in public speech – both texts explore that voice's subversive ability to point out publicly the self-serving interests unacknowledged by, because threatening to, those who control public culture.

Both Pierre Glendinning and Orville Deville, the male protagonists of *Pierre* and *The Fatal Marriage*, though on the verge of manhood, remain in upper-class homes ruled by women invested in impeding their maturation by controlling their sexuality. Though Lady Elizabeth Deville and Mrs. Glendinning seem to encourage their sons' acquisition of the privileges of upper-class manhood, both women's overweening love masks their desire to make permanent their temporary control over the vast estates through which the women wield public as well as familial power. Orville's mother, Lady Elizabeth Deville, asserts that her "one predominant affection" is "maternal love" (94). "Her one ruling passion [being] her son," Lady Deville's "devotion to him reached idolatry" (94). Mrs. Glendinning likewise finds in her "reverential and devoted son . . . lover enough," despite being "a lady who externally furnished a singular example of the preservative and beautifying influences of unfluctuating rank, health, and wealth" (24).

The mothers' passionate affections cause them to plan adult erotic relationships for their sons that will ensure their own emotional and practical hegemony over Orville and Pierre and the estates the men will inherit. Though in retrospect Mrs. Glendinning rejoices that Pierre's "little wife, that is to be, will not estrange him from me," and is grateful that "[he] loves her so and not some . . . haughtiness with whom I could never live in peace" (41), Lady Elizabeth takes a more premeditated role in channeling her son's desire. At her brother's deathbed in Scotland, she arranges and has executed the marriage of her twelve-year-old niece, Adelaide, to fifteen-year-old Orville, and so imagines that "the great dread of her future – a daughter-in-law to make her miserable" – has been averted. In the years between the marriage and its consummation, Orville goes to Eton while Lady Elizabeth takes Adelaide to Riverview, the family seat, in order to "melt, mould, and shape her into a perfect model of a wife for her darling son – a perfect pattern of a daughter-in-law for herself" (94). Upon Orville's return, Lady Elizabeth attempts to solidify her centrality in the sexual relationship that she imagines is about to commence by reminding her son that "in your great happiness do not utterly forget your mother whose care has secured you your greatest blessing" (125). Thus, in both texts the maternal solicitude that supposedly defines the private sphere[38] cloaks a lust for patriarchal power that finally blurs reigning nineteenth-century distinctions between the public and private, masculinity and femininity.

Though both mothers are confident that their positions not only in their sons' esteem, but in the patriarchies the men will acquire with their impending majority, are ensured by Orville's and Pierre's choice of sexual partners, neither woman can ultimately control the nature of her son's interest in women. Both Orville and Pierre secretly become fascinated with women whose radical dissimilarity to the erotic choices provided for them is signified most profoundly by the women's relationship to speech. The meekness that makes Adelaide and Lucy so desirable to the men's mothers is evidenced by their speech as well as by their manners. While Lucy is "noiseless . . . except with Pierre; and even with him she lives through many a panting hush" (47), Adelaide has "smiling lips," "balmy breath," and a "holy voice." Though Lucy's and Adelaide's speech exemplifies nineteenth-century linguistic paradigms of women's language,[39] Pierre and Orville are attracted to Isabel and Lionne because of the women's wild and disconcerting voices. "Ominously heralded by lightning and thunder," as well as by her "huntsman's horn" with its "clear, sweet, short notes of the recall" (27), Lionne arouses Orville's interest by the sounds preceding and emanating from her. When she finally does break "upon his sight" (28), uttering "picturesque and poetic language [that] was as strange to him as every other circumstance relating to her" (33), Orville is convinced that she is "beautiful, beyond possibility of comparison with any woman whom he had ever before gazed upon" (28). Pierre is similarly transfixed by a woman whose voice seems only "incidentally embodied" (73). Envisioning a woman's face that "without one word of speech" is able to "reveal glimpses of some fearful gospel" (67), Pierre later hears "a sudden, long-drawn, unearthly, girlish shriek" (69), which he imagines to come from the face. Unable to see "the person from whom it came," Pierre is all the more moved by the disembodied voice that "seemed to split its way clean through his heart, and leave a yawning gap there" (69). It is because he encounters the face and the voice separately that each influences him so profoundly. Acknowledging belatedly that "the long-drawn, unearthly, girlish shriek [that] pealed through and through his soul . . . came from the face . . . that wrought upon him" (73), Pierre's extended interest in Isabel is produced by the tenuous relationship that continues to exist between her voice and body.

As they listen to the content of the women's subsequent talk about the effects of male independence from the domestic sphere, the men recognize as grasping their mothers' attempts to confine them to the family circle in order to maintain control over their patrilineal inheritance.[40] "Forgotten by her father," who remains absent, "buried in his dreams and schemes and correspondence – political, radical, revolutionary" (67), Lionne describes to Orville her resulting sense of profound dispossession. Alienated from experiences that in retrospect seem "like glimpses of a pre-existence, seen in dreams, or like descriptions read in books" (60), Lionne continues to feel isolated and displaced even in the "mountain lodge, where [she has] been living eight or nine years" (60). Acknowledging that she feels without "a friend or companion in the wide, wide, world" (62), Lionne describes her alienation with the words that in the 1850s most powerfully signify young women's experience of psychological disorientation and crisis because of family dissolution.[41]

Likewise asking Pierre for "pity, pity" as she "freeze[s] in the wide, wide, world" (89), Isabel describes a past life in which "real things" are indistinguishable from "the unrealest dreams" (145). As she tells of the isolation and neglect she experienced as a child because of her father's abandonment, Isabel convinces Pierre of a consanguinity that radically alters his recollection of his father's relation to the domestic arena. Reviewing a hitherto unrecognizable portrait of Mr. Glendinning in light of this new information, Pierre imagines that it confesses to being "thy father as he more truly was" (109). Isabel's physical resemblance to this unfamiliar, "strangely translated" (139) image of his father thus transforms Pierre's understanding of men's relation to the domestic sphere and of the women who inhabit it.

By combining, rather than replacing, the content of these accounts with the remarkable tone in which the women speakers relate them, both men are able to feel desire for the women that allows them to frustrate their mothers' attempts to supplant their power. However, unlike the listeners in the preceding chapter, these men's attraction depends upon, and is a direct reaction to, the content as much as the tone of the women's voices. Initially enticed by "her innocent disclosures" (41), Orville is finally forced to admit that it is Lionne's "tones [that] have power to thrill my whole nature" (72). Commenting on the vocal tone that he finds sexually appealing, Orville asks, "Is the voice of the river so musical? I do not know, for the supernal melody of *one* voice has spoiled me for all others!" (36). Once confronted with the "sweet, wild power of the musicalness of [her] voice" (140), Pierre likewise experiences sensory and erotic stimulation that transforms the "life which he had vowed to Lucy" (78). As Isabel reveals the "inmost tones of [her] heart's deepest melodies" (141) to Pierre, he immerses himself in those "low melodies of her far interior voice" as they hover "in sweet echoes in the room" (145). Creating a sexual attraction unimaginable, according to the narrator, had Isabel been "a humped, and crippled, hideous girl" (135), the "low, sweet, half-sobbing voice of more than natural musicalness" combined with Isabel's beautiful "face ... mutely mournful" (135) causes Pierre to experience for the first time the sexual impulses that are "the inevitable ... lot of ... men" (135).

Marrying the women they so desperately want,[42] as we have seen before, enables men anxious about their power to assert their dominance – in this case over the mothers who advocate sexual relationships in order to extend their authority into the male arena. Orville returns to River-view and, though he does not disclaim his marriage to Adelaide, he refuses to consummate it "because of the fetter of sin that binds" him (147). Hoping to overcome Orville's sexual abstinence, Lady Elizabeth lures him into Adelaide's bedroom and demands that he sit beside her on Adelaide's couch. Acting as a stand-in for his wife, to which Lady Elizabeth takes this opportunity to remind him he has a sexual right, she achieves her goal of overcoming his palpable sexual anxiety and bringing "him through that communicating [bedroom] door" (146) for the first time. Yet Orville's prior sexual encounter fortifies him to withstand even this maternal onslaught, and though he acknowledges to himself that "he might have *a legal privilege*, . . . he felt that he had *no moral right* to enter there! . . . he . . . felt as uncomfortable, as much out of his sphere, as a sinner might feel in heaven!" (146). Pierre's precipitous marriage to Isabel similarly allows him to defend himself against the sexual alliance his mother self-servingly promotes, and Lucy's bedroom likewise becomes the space in which Pierre articulates his resistance. Entering Lucy's bedroom as she sleeps, Pierre "advance[s] slowly and deliberately toward her" in order "to pronounce to her her fate" (214–15). Pierre's declaration to Lucy that he is married precedes and so reinforces his disclosure to his mother. After hearing Pierre's admission, Mrs. Glendinning immediately asks if he has told Lucy. Pierre's positive reply finalizes the breach between both Lucy and Pierre and Mrs. Glendinning and her son.

"EVERYTHING TO AVENGE"

Orville and Pierre rely on both the content and tone of Lionne's and Isabel's voices in order to recognize and curb their mothers' appropriation of their patrilineal power, but the women's subsequent speech about men's illicit sexuality affects, in ways the men cannot control, their position in the public arena. Though neither Orville nor Pierre imagines that his illegitimate marital alliance will jeopardize his social position, neither man can control the effect of the women's voices once they infiltrate the public arenas over which the men preside. While Lionne's disembodied speech, as we will see later, enters the public sphere in which Orville wields the power enjoyed by the Devilles in order to divest him of it, Isabel's voice, once reinforced by her guitar, produces a public narrative through Pierre that destroys his social privilege. Isabel's guitar both corroborates her story and amplifies her oddly disembodied voice. Asserting that she knew from the first time she saw it that "there was melodiousness lurking in the thing . . . that the guitar was speaking to me" (153–4), Isabel goes on to describe the role that the talking guitar plays in her discovery of her mother and patrilineage. Because "all the wonders that are unimaginable and unspeakable; all these wonders are translated in the mysterious melodiousness of the guitar" (154), Isabel discovers the personal identity denied her by a society unwilling to acknowledge the illegitimate offspring of its upper-class men. She demonstrates the guitar's vocal power by having it "sing to thee the sequel of my story; for not in words can it be spoken" (154). While the guitar produces "low, sweet, and changefully modulated notes" without being touched, it more specifically "breathe[s] the word *mother*" (178) and so in both its tone and content verifies Isabel's account of her identity. This second disembodied voice, once it combines with and reinforces Isabel's, overwhelms Pierre, who is "bewitched" and "enchanted" by "first the enigmatical story of the girl . . . [the] haziness, obscurity and almost miraculousness of it . . . and then, the inexplicable spell of the guitar, and the subtleness of the melodious appealings of the few brief words from Isabel sung in the conclusion of the melody" (156).

Profoundly affected by the "mystical," diffuse speech of Isabel and her guitar, Pierre fashions his revisionist account of bourgeois, male sexuality on the stories they tell. His memory jogged by Isabel's speech, Pierre suddenly recalls incidents from his childhood that shed "another twinkling light upon her history" (166) and by extension on his own. While the "mystical corroborations in his own mind . . . substantiat[e]" (166) Isabel's story, they also disclose a repressed family history of duplicitous male sexuality that produces both Isabel and the ostracism she describes. Though Mrs. Glendinning asserts that her husband "was profoundly in love" with her, Pierre suddenly remembers his aunt's account of the impassioned relationship with a foreign woman of unknown class that preceded his father's more "suitable and excellent" (101) match with his mother. Confronted by the supposed offspring of this union, Pierre is forced to recognize not only the advantage to which his father put his class and sexual privilege, but the "pride of birth . . . affluence . . . and purity" (115) that keeps his mother from recognizing the sexual predatoriness of upper-class men like her husband. His own desire for Isabel corroborating the disorderliness of his father's sexuality, Pierre suddenly "catch[es] glimpses, and seem[s] to half see, somehow, that the uttermost ideal of moral perfection in man is wide of the mark" (310). Deciding to "write such things . . . [to] gospelize the world anew, and show them deeper secrets than the Apocalypse" (310), Pierre begins a writing career inspired by Isabel's voice and the story it tells. Relying on both, Pierre has Isabel play "her mystic guitar till [he feels] chapter after chapter born of its wondrous suggestiveness" (320).

Yet because both the tone and content of his descriptions of bourgeois male sexual consciousness are structured by Isabel's speech, his narrative destroys Pierre's elite position in the public arena he tries to refashion. In the process of analyzing middle-class society, Pierre's own position within it shifts. Because his writing focuses on a subject both socially seditious and "eternally incapable of being translated into words" (320), Pierre and his book are banned from polite society. Pierre learns that the Glendinning's rank is not innate, but the product of social and economic forces that are regulated by the community he criticizes. Though he "determine[s] at all hazards to hold his father's [name] inviolate from any thing he should do" (203), Pierre's literary career destroys not only his own social and economic status but finally the Glendinning line. Forcing his sole male relative to retract his slanderous words by returning the written version of them wrapped around a bullet, Pierre "slaughter[s] the only unoutlawed human being by the name of Glendinning" and so with "his own hand . . . extinguishe[s] his house" (402) in its entirety as well as the patriarchy associated with it.

While Isabel's account of men's illicit sexuality works through Pierre to displace the Glendinning men from the public sphere, Lionne maintains control of her own voice and speech, maximizing the power of its discrete relation to her body in order to compel an unrepenting Orville to acknowledge his seduction publicly. While the first section of *The Fatal Marriage* details the effect of Orville's secret marriage on his status within the Deville household, the rest of the text focuses on the identification and public dissemination of his action. Once Orville returns to River-view, he wonders, appalled, "*What had he done? . . .* He dared not answer his own question! He shrank shuddering from the thought of *the name that the law would have given his crime*" (111). The question "*What had he done?*" (121) and the response, "*A felony to which he dared not give its legal name*" (127), register the action that is unspeakable in the upper-class domestic world he reenters and become refrains validating the subsequent actions of Lionne. While Orville hopes to leave his "crime" unnamed, Lionne manipulates the relation between her body and voice in order to disseminate an account of Orville's sexual past that finally forces him to surrender his "natural" position within the upper echelons of the public arena.

Lionne's dramatic claim that she has "EVERYTHING TO AVENGE!" – uttered in a "low, deep, steady, [and] terrible tone" (229) – epitomizes her strategic vocal interventions in the public gatherings over which Orville presides. Because of Orville's seduction, Lionne has been deprived not only of the Deville name, but of her father's name and estate as well, which Orville, as his nephew, inherits. Thinking Lionne dead, her father, now restored to his Scottish earldom, toasts Orville and Adelaide as the "next Earl and Countess of Glen Lennark" at a banquet held in their honor. Yet the response, "*Lady Glen Lennark accedes and thanks your courtesy!*" (349–50), comes "not from the rosy lips of Adelaide" but from an unlocated, "deep-toned solemn, vibrating voice that tolled like a death bell through the room" (250). Responding to Orville's demand to know "Who spoke?" Lionne's disembodied voice answers, "*Leonora, Countess of Glen Lennark and Baroness Lockburn*" (350), and so publicly dispossesses Orville of the Glen Lennark estate. While Orville does "as the awful voice commanded," "leav[ing] title, castle, and estate" (356) out of a "secret, unconscious regard for his imperilled honour," he is enraged by the realization that while "the spring of wealth, rank and honour [are] within his reach," Lionne's voice alone is enough "to deprive him of rank, honor and liberty" (357).

Not content to reclaim from Deville her title and inheritance, Lionne continues to intrude in the public ceremonies that mark Orville's political and familial rites of passage in order to destroy both his personal and professional life. At the christening of the Devilles' first child, for example, "a deep, bell-toned, authoritative voice" breaks into the communal prayer in order to proclaim that "the first-born daughter of Orville Deville is beyond your prayers" (361). "The tremendous effect [of] this horrible speech, uttered as it was, by the hollow voice of an invisible speaker" (379), devastates Adelaide, who becomes so obsessed with the disembodied voice that she cannot control her own talk about it. Even after she once again becomes silent about the voice, Adelaide remains incapable of "banish[ing] it from my *mind* as from my *tongue*" (363). The speech that Lionne directly exchanges with Adelaide initially destroys Orville's domestic happiness. Crushed by proof that Orville indulges in the sexual practices available to men of his class, Adelaide refuses to consummate their marriage. However, as she hears Lionne describe the active sexuality defining her prior marriage to Orville and culminating in her pregnancy, Adelaide begins to experience a profound sexual desire absent from her earlier relations with Orville.[43] Yet, while the "pure, calm, trusting love of years had been by grief sublimed to passion" (273), the grief that inspires her desire continues to check its consummation. Recognizing "the consuming passion of her heart" (273), Orville presses "his lips with devouring avidity to her" (274), but Lionne's vocal intrusion into their bedchamber, coupled with the strain that their mutual passion exerts on Adelaide's body, causes Adelaide to collapse, and their attempt to consummate their marriage is again foiled. Seeking solace for his troubled marriage in a public career, Orville turns to politics, and "because of his high rank, ample fortune, splendid talents, and not too scrupulous honour . . . he was elected to the House of Assembly" (408). Contemplating the restorative effect of his election on his marriage, Orville is "just about to open his mouth to commence" his political acceptance speech when he is again publicly silenced

54

by "the single word LIONNE – that tolled like a death-bell through the room" (411).

Foiled at every stage by Lionne's unlocatable public speech, Orville finally acknowledges both publicly and privately his sexual criminality. Breaking the long domestic silence about his seduction of Lionne, Orville tells Adelaide that "the time has come when all concealments . . . must be at an end" (456). Foregrounding his confession to Adelaide by acknowledging that "Lionne . . . told . . . nothing but the truth, truth until now unacknowledged by me," Orville insists on telling Adelaide his story in full detail, rather than continuing to base their discussion upon her "conjecture as though it had been a mutually recognized truth" (457). The importance that he ascribes to naming the events surrounding his marriage to Lionne leads Orville to use for the first time the legal term for his action, when he admits to Adelaide that "the certificate of my – yes! I will speak the fatal word – *felonious* marriage with herself is in her possession" (458). That certificate forces Orville to accept the public as well as private sentence for bigamy. During his trial, the success of Orville's "not guilty" plea depends on convincing the jury that his offense was "the act of youthful passion and folly" and not "a felony, since *intention* constitutes the crime" (479). While "few present looked for other than a full acquittal for the accused," his plea is overridden by "one tremendous word from the foreman of the jury," which, in language reminiscent of Lionne's, "fell like a thunderbolt upon the accused. That word of doom was – 'GUILTY' " (481). And so, finally, Lionne's vocal tone and content, because dissociated from her body, compel Orville to answer publicly the question that she first poses to him: "If Adelaide is your wife – *what then is Lionne?*" (129).

In both *The Fatal Marriage* and *Pierre*, female speech reveals women's desire for public privilege and men's marginality to the public sphere. Both texts thus radically challenge the "natural" gender distinctions that characterize middle-class life. Contemporary reading audiences and reviewers responded to both novels in much the same way that Southworth and Melville depicted fictional audiences as doing, thereby reinforcing both writers' association between the disembodied voice and the narratives that feature them. Contemporary reviews of *Pierre,* much like the public's response to Pierre's text, decried the author's revisionist project. Claiming that Melville had lost his mind, these reviewers called the novel a "monstrous," "unhealthy," and "improper work" because it exposed the underside of "universally-received rules of moral and social order."[44] By denouncing the novel, critics hoped to ensure that it, along with its criticism of "the holy relations of the family" (42), would remain "shrouded in a decorous darkness" (60). Conversely, critics of *The Fatal Marriage,* like the public that finally condemned Orville for his bigamous marriage, consistently lauded the novel for upholding woman's "chasteness and purity"[45] and declared the text important reading for women of all ages. However dissimilar the receptions of *Pierre* and *The Fatal Marriage,* reading the two texts together, as literary scholars suggest, proves useful, for doing so reveals their shared interest in reimagining the relation between the female voice and body in order to bolster the political impact of that voice and by extension the narratives that feature it. By depicting women who effectively communicate detailed accounts of men's illicit sexual behavior to resisting audiences and thereby upset the control of such men over the public arena, as well as their preeminence within it, both Southworth and Melville alter the linguistic consensus that American women's voices, because of their purity, elevate but are incapable of directly engaging in and contributing to public debate. Exploring the implications of transcendentalists' contention that the content and tone of women's speech must reflect all aspects of their social and sexual lives, *Pierre* and *The Fatal Marriage* show how women's sexually explicit speech destabilizes bourgeois constructions of gender and language and thereby reshapes the public sphere in which middle-class ideology is enforced. Thus, with their depictions of women's voices and their radical public speech, both novels in turn become influential acts of public speech that encourage us to reconsider prevailing accounts of American women's speech in the twentieth as well as in the nineteenth century.

3

Incarnate Words

Nativism, Nationalism, and the Female Body in
Maria Monk's *Awful Disclosures*

In the preceding chapter we saw how writers use the female voice and the public speech it generates in order to launch a powerful critique of nineteenth-century middle-class culture. By engaging in the wide range of political discussions that sustained the public sphere throughout the century, the woman-authored novels that I treat in the following chapters challenge bourgeois notions of the separate spheres of influence. However, all of these texts enhance their rhetorical power and so their political impact by depicting the complex relation between the female voice and women's public speech. Each of the political movements I survey invokes in one way or another the female voice as a part of its political rhetoric, but the novels that contribute to these debates include in their depictions of the female voice its influence on women's public speech. In so doing, they remind readers of the cultural significance that, as I have shown, accrues to the female voice in nineteenth-century America and thereby maximize the impact of their public political discourse. In subsequent chapters I will explore women writers' contributions to the labor reform, pro-slavery, abolition, and woman's suffrage movements, but in the following pages I want to assess the nature of Maria Monk's profound effect on the nativist movement and related discourses of nationalism.

American Anti-Catholicism

The anti-Catholic movement in nineteenth-century America initially developed in reaction to the dramatic increases in immigration beginning in the 1830s, primarily from Roman Catholic Ireland, but the movement gained political force in the three decades preceding the Civil War. Because the anti-Catholic or nativist movement reimagined the nation as originally peopled with "native" or "pure" Americans, and as only suddenly threatened by immigrants' invasions of its boundaries, it held particular appeal for a nation increasingly aware of the regional and racial conflicts burgeoning within its borders.[1] As the anonymous author of the nativist tract *Sons of the Sires* (1855) argues, early immigrants to the United States "were men who . . . contributed to the strength and wealth of the nation" and so "were essentially different in their principles and character" from the "idlers," "paupers," and "criminals" "who now form the unbroken current which is pouring its millions upon our soil."[2] By making dramatic distinctions between "native" (or at least third-generation) Americans and inferior, invasive outsiders, nativists externalized the nation's conflicts and consolidated its sense of national identity.

The Awful Disclosures of the Hotel Dieu Nunnery (1836), Maria Monk's purportedly autobiographical account of her experiences in a convent, generated crucial and as yet unexplored momentum in the early stages of this nativist movement. Written after her escape from the Hotel Dieu, Monk's text describes in detail her brief life as a nun and the tortures she saw Catholic practitioners inflict on women's bodies. With its gruesome account of women's daily exploitation and oppression under a Catholic regime, *Awful Disclosures* provoked such intense ethnocentrism and religious intolerance among its readers that they demanded public inspections of convents, public meetings featuring Monk, and sequels to her original text. Yet, despite its immense political sway in the years preceding the Civil War[3] and its undisputed status as "the greatest of the nativistic propaganda works,"[4] Monk's text has only recently begun to attract scholarly interest. Barbara Welter has suggested that this history of critical avoidance is the result of the violently exclusionary and prejudicial politics of the nativist movement.[5] Within the past ten years, however, associations in feminist political theory between nationalism and the female body have provided a new critical framework within which to analyze Monk's text. Lynn Hunt, for example, has pointed out the ways in which the female body came to signify the national body in Europe during such political upheavals as the French Revolution.[6] From such accounts we can see how members of the nativist movement, because of their abiding concern for the increasing permeability of America's borders, became particularly susceptible to the iconographic power of the sexually vulnerable American female body. Thus, as I will show, one of the reasons that the sexually endangered women in Monk's text provoke overwhelming nativist sentiment is that they embody many Americans' fears about immigrants' effects on the integrity of the nation.

Influenced by such nativist figurations of the nation, existing assessments of Monk's work have tended to turn to Monk's sexual history to determine the accuracy of her account of women's sexual violation. For example, in *Roads to Rome: The Antebellum Protestant Encounter with Catholicism* (1994), Jenny Franchot invokes as R. A. Billington did fifty years earlier, the autobiographical details of Monk's life – her unwanted pregnancy, estrangement from her mother, and final prostitution – to render "incredible" the fact that "thousands of Americans believed Monk's narrative."[7] Carleton Beals, in *Brass-Knuckle Crusade* (1960), provides the most dramatic example of this critical conflation of narrative with writer. Arguing that Monk is a "little nymphomaniac," Beals's account of her text lapses into the sexually explicit narrative for which he criticizes Monk. Surrounded by "men of God" who "cluster-about to hear her sensational story," Monk, according to Beals, lies on a birthing bed, "close to her time, her large breasts half showing under her bed jacket," and tells her story.[8] By linking textual production to physical reproduction, Beals provides a striking example of scholars' enduring impulse, when assessing Monk's work, to interpret the one within the context of the other. Considering this tendency to turn to the narrator's body to find evidence of narrative "truth," Susan Griffin has recently determined that it is a strategy encouraged by and foregrounded in Monk's text and convent narratives in general.[9]

However, important as the female body is in *Awful Disclosures* for producing both nativist sentiment and critical commentary, the full political significance of Monk's narrative – how it defines twenty years of innovative nativist political rhetoric[10] and complicates current paradigms of nineteenth-century American female iconography – becomes apparent only once we acknowledge the complex relation within the text between women's bodies and the voices and public speech that emanate from them. Thus, by focusing exclusively on the female body, current accounts of *Awful Disclosures* give us only a partial picture of the text's political power in nineteenth-century American culture. In the narrative, women's voices do not represent and reinforce the social norms of the emerging middle class, but rather illustrate the profound threat that Catholicism poses to those standards. Monk depicts convent women's sexual exploitation as a series of constraints and assaults on their voices and then shows how Catholicism stifles women's attempts to speak publicly about such abuse.[11] According to the narrator, it is having witnessed the strict, repressive control that the convent exerts over women's voices and the way in which it silences women's public speech that motivates the writing of *Awful Disclosures*. Such attention to women's voices and public speech enables Monk to produce an account of Catholicism powerful enough to determine the form that nativist rhetoric would take in subsequent decades. By projecting her own public speech, via narrative, into the public sphere of the 1830s, Monk creates a demand for her own public appearance and speech within that political arena. In so doing she complicates current accounts of the nineteenth-century American woman's political power, which contend that the female icon's power derives from her "silence" and lack of "sexuality and passion."[12] However, in order to see the full magnitude of Monk's impact on both nativist propaganda and female iconography in the nineteenth century we must first assess anti-Catholic rhetoric and its reliance on the American woman's body.

From Virgin Soil to "Soiled" Virgin

Throughout the nineteenth century, many social commentators consistently voice their concern over the negative impact that the dramatic increase in immigration will have on the linguistic superiority that defines both the nation and American women. Speaking, I showed in Chapter 1, for the vast majority of language theorists, James Fenimore Cooper proclaims in *The American Democrat* (1838) that, because women have "the highest quality of eloquence," they are "the natural agents in maintaining the refinement" of American English.[13] Yet the women who immigrate to the United States, according to Otto Jesperson, "remain more within doors" and therefore "keep the old . . . language" intact, which will have an adverse effect on the English language and the women who maintain it.[14] William Dean Howells asserts that the "women of inferior nationalities" who are streaming into the country must have their speech monitored. According to Howells, "The Italians . . . have speaking voices notoriously shrill and harsh," while "the throats of the Spanish, thickened by their gutturals, do not emit the clear and sweet notes of their more northern sisters." While "the Frenchwomen speak sweetly, and from their throats in spite of a language whose abounding nasals invite them to employ their noses" and "the Germans, whose speech deforms their mouths, have yet a soft and musical enunciation," the American woman's voice is unequivocally superior.[15] Thus, Henry James, in his address to Bryn Mawr College graduates, warns American women to protect themselves and their speech against "the vast contingent of aliens whom we make welcome, and whose main contention . . . is that, from the moment of their arrival, they have just as much property in our speech as we have."[16]

To persuade their audiences that America's linguistic and thus national identity is threatened by the Catholicism of a swelling immigrant population, nativists overwhelmingly depict the United States as a pure woman with elevated speech. In *Immigration: Its Evils and Consequences* (1856), nativist Samuel Busey asserts that the unified "identity of the population of . . . [the] country is essential to the preservation of good order, to the perpetuity of its established institutions, and to the protection of its citizens," but he concludes that the recent influx of immigrants is destroying the ideological and physical unity of America's citizens.[17] To convince their audiences that immigrants are threatening the integrity of America's geographic and ideological boundaries, nativists figure the country as one of its female citizens. Maria McIntosh, for example, pointedly asks the readers of *Woman in America: Her Work and Her Reward* (1850), "Do you really value your country, her freedom, her intelligence?" If they do, she demands that they "awake . . . and see how the darkness from other lands is overshadowing her intelligence – how the oppressed multitudes of other nations, escaping from their galling bonds, threaten . . . to trample [her] freedom underfoot."[18] While McIntosh imagines the nation to be a woman, Anna Carroll more specifically begins the chapter entitled "The Men of America" in her popular nativist tract, *The Great American Battle* (1859), by depicting America's literal birth as both a nation and a woman. Writing that "with irresistible will America . . . started into life; . . . she opened her young arms to mankind, and offering them her life, her truth . . . called all men brethren," Carroll not only figures the nation as a woman, but defines its relation to the "men of America" as familial and platonic.[19] Because of her sisterly relation to all of her men, America is prototypical of the "passionless" women who, according to Nancy Cott, increasingly came to represent middle-class womanhood in the nineteenth century.[20] This passionlessness also clarifies America's reliance on men. The iconographic America is emblematic of her womenfolks' "stern virtue," but she is also vulnerable to attacks upon that virtue, and thus dependent on her men for protection (Carroll, 14).

Nativists also characterize America as sexually and ideologically under attack by the Catholics penetrating her borders. Though America has been "the foster-mother that shelters and nourishes those outcasts who fled to her bosom for protection" (*Sons,* 9) she is suddenly threatened by the very individuals she succors. The author of *The Sons of the Sires,* identifying himself only as "an American," compels his readers to envision the effects of unchecked Catholicism on both the nation and the identity of its future citizens when he asks, "Shall we see a many-headed monster springing from the womb of the virgin of Liberty?" (19). The progeny from America's coupling with Catholicism not only signifies the "unnaturalness" of the union, but attests to the perceived perversity of Catholic sexuality in general. Thus, Carroll asserts that as a nation "we contend against a foe of feverish passions. . . . It is the Romish Hierarchy, the Jesuit Priesthood, the political church in America" (47). While George Mosse notes that "lack of control over their passions characterized all outsiders," Lynn Hunt specifies the particular susceptibility of European Catholics to accusations of sexual excess.[21] Ultimately fearing that Catholicism's uncontrollable and "unnatural" passion will transform America from virgin soil to soiled virgin, Carroll demands, "Is America to become the Sodom and Gomorrah for this machinery?" (48).

The threat that Catholicism poses to women's sexual purity as well as linguistic integrity in turn challenges and consolidates nationalistic notions of nineteenth-century American manhood. Claiming that historically "America was manned with that inextinguishable spirit of liberty, which would not suffer her to be smitten on the cheek, or hung between two dogs – and then ask are we men?" Carroll makes the physical vulnerability of the national female body explicit in order to highlight the responsibility accruing to men because of their masculinity (46). Thus endangered, America "calls aloud for . . . manly hearts to shiver off, to tear away, to fling afar, the source of these stifled groans and distressing sobs, which is taking all the lustre from her eye and paralyzing the very limbs of America" (42). If America's body is deteriorating, its impending dissolution offers men a prime opportunity to prove their patriotic "manliness." As Carroll exclaims, "Oh, what a moment for America's men, when their families, their wives and children, are endangered by an influence which impregnates her air, her temperature" (50). It is the direct effect of the sexually violated body of America on the women who inhabit her land that justifies the nationalistic and manly exertions of her male populace.

As Benedict Anderson argues, the nation is "imagined as a *commu-*

nity because, regardless of the actual inequality and exploitation that may prevail, . . . the nation is always conceived as a deep, horizontal comradeship," but that comradeship in the nativist movement is consolidated around the female body and the masculinity that its endangerment evokes in male citizens.[22] Noting that "America had her men. There was Washington . . . Madison, Hamilton, and Jay . . . when at Mount Vernon . . . the Constitution of the United States of America was conceived," Carroll argues that in the past "real" American men have controlled America's ideological as well as biological conceptions (44). She goes on to specify the kind of masculinity that allows "the breath, the energy . . . of true men" to "people" the nation (44), when she notes that America "wants all her men, every one of them; not crying men with pocket-handkerchiefs to their eyes, but men who decide all and are men" (51). Claiming that such men "are her national guard, her troops, her power, to hoist her flag when and where the nation wills it," Carroll suggests that they not only protect America's feminine virtue, but fetishistically empower her in turn to plant her own nationalist emblem in foreign soil (48). Yet, should they fail, America reserves the right to "reject and condemn the very men who gave the whole world America" (48).

Though nativist propaganda invokes the physical boundaries of a female America in order to bolster the masculinity of its male-dominated audience, its national political instrument, the Know-Nothing Party, figures itself as the male body that, because of its secrecy and lack of visible boundaries, is able to keep the nation's identity intact.[23] America's vulnerability to the phallic intrusions of a foreign power structures both the form and content of Lyman Beecher's nativist argument that "we, around the entire circumference of our nation, leave wide opened the door of entrance, and all the vital energies of our institutions, accessible to any influence which the anti-republican governments of Europe may choose to thrust in upon us."[24] In proclaiming itself the protector of this endangered America, the Know-Nothing Party imagines itself as just the kind of male that Carroll claims the nation needs. The author of *The Sons of the Sires* (1855) describes his party as "the child of the people . . . he is now a youth of rare capacities and of glorious promise . . . very much in appearance like the pictures of the manly Washington" (14). Because this manly nativist youth is clearly the purebred progeny of America's most vital men, he is immediately under Catholic attack, according to the narrator's story, and escapes his fate only by going into hiding. Resurfacing "yonder, and there, and everywhere," the youth emblematic of the Know-Nothing Party defies fixed physical boundaries in order to shore up America's geographic and ideological borders (11).

In *Awful Disclosures,* Maria Monk not only creates the nativist image of the sexually endangered woman but, as I have shown, ensures its subsequent centrality to the nativist movement. Her narrative achieved unprecedented success because it includes in its portrayal of violated female bodies assaults on the female voices that, as I have illustrated, were becoming important to the nation but that linguists feared would be contaminated by increased immigration. To influence her audience further, Monk depicts the female voice's contested relation to public speech. By showing how women who attempt to speak publicly about their vocal and bodily oppression are brutally silenced to enforce Catholic rather than bourgeois ideology, Monk encourages audiences that might categorically oppose women's political intervention to advocate for escaped nuns' public speech. Though Monk strategically claims that she writes her narrative to ensure that the stifled public speech of these women is heard and thus that Americans are alerted to the social and civic dangers that Catholicism poses, her narrative actually undermines the middle-class ideals it purports to uphold, first, because it contributes to the political discussion from which women are often barred and, second, because it creates a demand for Monk's own public appearance and speech. However, in order to see the full revisionist magnitude of Monk's text, we must assess how its depictions of Catholic women rely upon the female voice and its public speech, and thereby activate the cultural concerns surrounding both.

Breaking Silence

The convent looms large both in Monk's account and more generally in the minds of anti-Catholic nativists, because it remains entirely separate from and so insusceptible to the public opinion and scrutiny that regulate middle-class behavior. Its architectural structure reinforcing Catholicism's resistance to outside regulation, the convent becomes a symbol, for nativists, of the antisocial behavior they imagine goes on behind its walls. As one anonymous contributor to the *American Protestant Vindicator* (1836) imaginatively puts it, "Uncleanness and murder are the corner stones of the nunnery, . . . its walls are built up with the most heinous crimes, and the cement is the blood of innocence."[25] British diarist Frederick Marryat argues that Americans' anxious speculations about convent life grew out of a strong "national feeling that nothing must be kept veiled" and finally motivated the 1834 burning of the Ursuline convent in Boston. "Americans," he writes in *Diary in America* (1839), "cannot bear anything like a secret – that's *unconstitutional*," and so, because "the Convent was *sealed* to them," the Boston mob "determined to know what was in it" by storming it and burning it to the ground.[26] If Protestant Americans' anxiety about the convent derived from its physical position outside the purview of public surveillance that Foucault has claimed produces, interprets, and controls sexual activity, Monk's text provokes its audience by emphasizing the unmonitored, sordid sexuality practiced behind the convent walls and so immune to public inspection.[27] Monk seeks narrative authority in her text by enjoining her audience to search the convent that she describes in order to verify the antisocial activities that she claims remain hidden within it. She asks her readers to provide a delegation to accompany her through the convent so "that they may compare my account with the interior parts of that building, into which no persons but the Roman Bishop and the Priests are ever admitted."[28] In so doing the narrator emphasizes the convent's essential impenetrability in order to provoke a predominantly Protestant public's anxiety about institutions both ideologically and architecturally resistant to the communal, Foucaultian policing that, according to cultural critics and historians, epitomized nineteenth-century American culture.[29]

Because the convent resists public scrutiny and social control, nativists fear the resulting power of Catholicism's main mode of surveillance – the confessional. Lyman Beecher articulates a general nativist concern when, in *A Plea for the West* (1835), he writes that "by the confessional [Catholicism] searches the heart, learns the thoughts, and motives, and habits, and condition of individuals and families, and thus acquires the means of unlimited ascendancy over the mind by the united influence of both worlds" (132). In the minds of nativists, its dual access to both the public and private worlds of its parishioners and its lack of public accountability combine to make confession the most dangerous Catholic practice. Nativists consistently imagine that its ritualized dialogue authorizes deviant sexuality. In "The History of Priestcraft" (1837), for example, William Howitt asks his readers to imagine "the effect on domestic purity" of the "millions of monks and secular priests" who, "forbidden to marry" and "pampered in . . . voluptuousness," have been "let loose on the female world as counsellors and confessors."[30] "With secrecy in one hand, and amplest power of absolution from sin in the other," these priests, Howitt asserts, destroy the sexual purity of every woman who confesses to them.

In *Awful Disclosures* Monk describes the confessional as the physical space within the convent in which Catholic ideology is most effectively inculcated and sexual transgression is thus most overtly institutionalized. The narrator, Saint Eustace, first discovers the sexual politics of the confessional from a girlfriend, who tells her of "conduct . . . criminal and shameful" (27) by a priest during confession. Recalling that "these stories struck me with surprise at first," the narrator admits that after many confessions "I gradually began to feel differently, even supposing [the stories] true, and to look upon the priests as men incapable of sin" (29). It is only after attending confession and having her attitudes shaped by the priests that the narrator is inducted into the sexual license of the confessional. Thus, she notes that "it was not until I had been several times, that the priests became more and more bold, and were at length indecent in their questions and even in their conduct when I confessed to them" (29).

The privacy of the confessional makes it a place of extreme sexual exploitation, but in Monk's text and in the nativist rhetoric it generated that exploitation is depicted exclusively as restrictions on the female voice. In a special issue of the *American Protestant Vindicator* (1836) devoted to *Awful Disclosures,* an anonymous contributor, in describing convent life, asserts that "the first precept includes a death-like silence." Once the newly inducted nun learns to be silent, "she is initiated into the [convent's] mysteries . . . by the priest in the confession box. . . . Through the application of questions which inculcate ideas that gradually extirpate all modesty," this priest ensures the debasement of every nun who confesses to him (2–3). A source for this and numerous other exposés on convent life,[31] Monk's *Awful Disclosures* similarly describes how priests, while listening to the nuns confess, "put questions . . . which were often of the most improper and even revolting nature, naming crimes both unthought of and inhuman" (41–2). The priests' sexual license is not confined to their own articulations, but involves gaining control over the nuns' voices as well. Thus, while Monk's narrator, Saint Eustace, admits to hearing "from the mouths of the priests at confession what I cannot repeat," she also relates that "several females . . . have assured me, that they have repeatedly, and indeed regularly, been required to answer . . . questions, many of which present[ed] to the mind deeds which the most iniquitous and corrupt heart could hardly invent" (29). Simultaneously maintaining and disrupting the sanctity of the confessional, the narrator admits that "far more guilt was often incurred than pardoned; and crimes of a deep die were committed" (124). Though Saint Eustace reiterates her inability to "speak plainly on such a subject" (124), the confessional structure of her narrative, as Foucault has suggested, lends credence to the sexual activities to which she alludes. Admitting that, among the nuns waiting outside the confessional, "there was often a contest . . . to avoid entering the apartment as long as we could, endeavoring to make each other go first, as that was what most of us dreaded" (125), the narrator's recollection lends shape and substance to her accusations of sexual abuse.

If the priests' talk, from the hegemonic side of the confession screen, constitutes their female penitents' sexual exploitation, from the other side of the screen the nuns' ritualized responses and their enforced silence alike become definitive signs of their oppressive experience in the convent. While Saint Eustace's desire to learn a second language motivates her to join the convent, once she takes the veil, she finds that all unmonitored speech is disallowed by convent rules. Because "the preservation of silence was insisted upon most rigidly," the narrator finds that she is "never allowed to speak" freely (101). "Permitted to speak with each other only on such subjects as relate to the Convent, and all in the hearing of the old nuns" (35), newly inducted nuns are unable to communicate their fears and impressions to one another. If the old nuns notice the novices' surreptitious attempts to speak, they inform the transgressors that they "have broken silence," and thereby enforce the silence and vocal control of convent life. Beginning with the old nuns' declaration that "the Lord cometh," and their charges' prescribed response, "Let us go and meet him," the nuns' daily routine revolves exclusively around organized prayer, "silence-bells," sermons, singing, and lectures (64). Vocal surveillance extends even into the nuns' sleep: the narrator reports a "proneness to talk in our sleep" and "to hear the nuns repeat their prayers in the course of the night, as they frequently did in their dreams" (176). Enforced vocal conformity circumscribes women's personal thoughts as well. As the narrator admits, because they were "forbidden to converse freely" on their sexual exploitation, the nuns "thought but little about it" (185).

Any nuns who speak publicly against the constraints on their voices are subjected to punishments that distort and torture their resistant mouths. Having noted that she has "seen half a dozen [nuns] . . . gagged and bound at once," Saint Eustace discloses her own subjection "to the same state of involuntary silence. . . . My hands . . . tied behind me, and a gag put into my mouth, sometimes with such force and rudeness as to lacerate my lips and cause the blood to flow freely" (186). Saint Eustace admits that, during a particularly painful penance, "if I had not been gagged, I am sure I should have uttered awful screams" (200). To stress the physical cost of challenging the regulatory regime, the narrator describes the pain the gag inflicts as it is placed in the mouth:

> The rough gagging which I several times endured wounded my lips very much; for it was common . . . to thrust the gag hard against the teeth, and catch one or both the lips, which were sometimes cruelly cut. . . . A gag was once forced into my mouth which had a large splinter upon it, and this cut through my upper lip . . . leaving . . . a scar. (190)

Admitting that she has "seen the blood flowing" from the numerous female "mouths into which the gag was thrust" (186), the narrator reminds her readers that Catholic practices place the female body, as well as women's voices, in jeopardy.

Yet those women who do speak publicly against Catholic practices serve as inspirational mouthpieces of communal resistance, before they become examples that further compel the nuns' vocal submission. For instance, one evening, as the women prepare to sleep, the "usual silence" is disrupted by "the most piercing and heart-rending shrieks" from a newly inducted nun. The cries of the sexually assaulted woman produce a spontaneous and disorderly outcry from the usually silent sisters: "Every nun seemed to rise as if by one impulse, for no one could hear such sounds, especially in such total silence, without being greatly excited. A general noise succeeded, for many voices spoke together, uttering cries of surprise, compassion, or fear . . . [and] for once we forgot rules and penances, and gave vent to our feelings" (149).

While one woman's involuntary enunciation of her fear activates the spontaneous vocal response of the other women, Saint Frances, another newly inducted nun, threatens the entire structure of institutionalized oppression by publicly speaking out against her vocal and sexual subordination. Saint Frances is on trial as much for her physical resistance as for her vocal disapproval of the convent's sexual practices. Dragged from her room, Saint Frances, "without even speaking a word," submits to the harsh speech that sets the tone for her punishment (113). Yet, if "Saint Frances spoke not a word" (114) on the way to her hearing, her speech once there proves disorderly. She repeats her vocal unruliness publicly, and "in reply to some . . . questions . . . she was silent; to others I heard her voice reply that she did not repent of the words she had uttered" (115). Though the Superior and priests gag Saint Frances to ensure her silence, her words prove inspirational for the nuns and particularly for Saint Eustace, who admits that her speech "made a lasting impression on me" (115).

Having depicted Catholicism's tyrannical control over the female voice and its overt silencing of women's subversive public speech, Monk goes on to show how it uses the vocal unruliness and public speech of one nun to consolidate its power. While initially seeming to resist oppression, the disorderly speech of the narrator's friend and confidante, Jane Ray, finally reaffirms the pervasiveness of Catholicism's hegemony. Jane sets "at nought . . . the rules of silence, which others were so scrupulous in observing" (137). She not only "speaks aloud when silence [is] required" but encourages vocal unruliness in the other nuns by saying and doing "things on purpose to make us laugh" (37). Thus, the narrator recollects:

> Often, while perfect silence prevailed among the nuns, . . . Jane would break forth with some remark or question that would attract general attention, and often cause a long and total interruption . . . her loud and well known voice, so strongly associated with everything singular and ridiculous, would arrest the attention of us all, and generally incline us to smile, and even force us to laugh. . . . I have repeatedly known her to break silence in the community, as if she had no object, or none beyond that of causing disturbance. (108)

Jane's language encourages the corresponding and irrepressible speech of her peers, but her tricks also cause the old nuns to scream inadvertently and so to find themselves accused of "breaking the silence" they are in charge of enforcing (134). While the disorderly speech that Jane provokes leaves all the other nuns vulnerable to censure, she is judged by the Superior to be incapable of controlling her irresponsible talk, and therefore is not held accountable for it.

Occupying the privileged position of a madwoman, Jane continues to use her voice to subvert the religious language and ideology of the convent. Because she speaks both French and English, she is charged with teaching novices the "official church language." Instead, she uses her bilingualism to attack the convent's vocal regimes and inculcates "irreverent passages from songs" (142). Jane not only teaches the nuns a subversive religious language, but creates a parodic version of the religious words they are forced to speak in order to give the nuns a way of articulating their feelings. Fixing on the Canadian nuns' slight deviation from prescribed speech, Jane repeats their term "for the God" until it becomes a code phrase the nuns use to express their disdain for convent rituals. Jane also publicly articulates the emotions the nuns are afraid to express. Because she is particularly resistant to confession, Jane decides to write rather than recite her confession. Yet, as she reads it before the Superior and all of the nuns, it becomes clear that "it was full of offenses which she had never committed, evidently written to throw ridicule on confessions" (139). Because of the unique role of Jane's speech in the convent, she not only is able to parody with impunity the Catholic practice most feared by the other nuns, but also becomes the communal spokesperson for the nuns' anxiety about the prolonged absence of their Superior. Thus, intimating "her own suspicions more plainly than any other of the nuns would have dared to do," Jane "spoke out one day . . . and said 'I'm going to have a hunt in the cellar for my old Superior' " (180). Her unusually beautiful singing voice reinforces the defiant content of her words. As Saint Eustace reports, Jane had "a very fine voice, which was so powerful as to be heard above the rest." She uses it publicly to oppose the religious singing in which the Superior forces her to take part. Thus, "sometimes she would be silent when other nuns began; and the Superior would often call out 'Jane Ray, you do not sing' . . . she would then strike up some English song, or profane parody, rendered ten times more ridiculous by the ignorance of the Lady Superior" (163), who speaks only French.

Though Jane criticizes repressive Catholic practices, she also serves an important function in ensuring the nuns' compliance. Jane's vocal antics disrupt the linguistic rituals of the convent, but they also maintain the nuns' spirits and so complicity in those rituals. Saint Eustace notes that "nothing but the humors of mad Jane Ray, could rouse us for a moment from our langor and melancholy" (125). As a result, she admits that she "was always inclined to think [the Superior] was willing to put up with some of her tricks, because they served to divert our minds from the painful and depressing circumstances in which we were placed" (136). Jane's vocal recuperation within the system of oppression that she resists is the final and most dramatic act of vocal appropriation in Monk's account and reveals the full extent of the convent's institutional hegemony. As a result, nativists imagine the Catholicism practiced in the convent as capable of destroying both the nation and the sexual and vocal integrity of the hardiest women who live in it.

Speaking Out

With this world of violent vocal surveillance as its subject, Monk's narrative becomes a dramatic example of breaking the silence of women both in the convent and in the nineteenth-century American political sphere. Though Jane Ray knows "everything" about the illicit practices of the convent because of her privileged position within it, Saint Eustace becomes, through conversation with Jane, "informed of scenes, supposed by the actors of them to be secret" (144). These scenes form the core of the narrative that Monk writes purportedly to ensure that, even if Jane is "silenced . . . before she has an opportunity to add her most important testimony" (13), her story will not be lost. Far from being lost, *Awful Disclosures* sold more than 20,000 copies within a few weeks of its publication and immediately became the best-selling, as well as the "most influential, single work of anti-Catholic propaganda in America's history" (Billington, 100). Because of the instant public interest that her account of convent women produced in her own body and voice, Monk entered the public sphere and transformed herself from a silent

American female icon into a nativist political orator. Her physical appearance as "an innocent young girl" (Beals, 3) first reinforced the veracity of her autobiographical narrative and then imbued her body with the iconographic power of the women in her text. Collapsing distinctions between Monk's own voice and the voices in the narrative, public audiences feared that the priests who had oppressed her in the convent would, according to the *American Protestant Vindicator* (1836), "obtain possession of Maria Monk, so as to inflict upon her the Papist gag law" (2). The iconographic power of Monk's body thus created, among audiences, a demand for the free and uninhibited female public speech that would reassure listeners that the nation, as well as the female body that represented it, remained intact.

While antebellum nativist rhetoric, as I have illustrated, made extensive use of Monk's iconographic paradigms, *Awful Disclosures* continued to influence immigration propaganda even after the nativist movement ended with the Civil War. Mary J. Holmes's pro-immigration novel, *The English Orphans* (1871), for example, employs the persuasive techniques originally set out in the pages of Monk's text. Like Jane Ray, Holmes's mad female character, Sal, has a "command of language" that is "proportionately greater" whenever she seems "crazier than usual."[32] Produced by the physical beatings and sexual oppression she suffers because of her immigrant status, the ironic "references to . . . grammar" (65) that denote Sal's insanity nonetheless protect and finally authorize the public speech of the novel's orphan heroine, Mary. Her own career as "a splendid minister . . . spoiled" (90), Sal devotes her energy to helping Mary overcome the tortured speech and distorted mouth that are her Catholic inheritance. Impaired by teeth "which, on each side of her mouth, grew directly over the others, giving to the lower portion of her face a peculiar and rather disagreeable expression" (8) and contort her voice, Mary epitomizes the "horridly miserable creatures" (20) of which anti-immigration proponents complain. Yet Sal's speech lessons and the operation that she underwrites transform Mary into an attractive, pure woman whose speech is powerful enough to repel the advances of intemperate and preda-

74

tory men. The political impact of Holmes's text is produced by Mary's metamorphosis from a silenced and sexually vulnerable orphan into a representative of passionless bourgeois femininity, but the full resonance of Mary's conversion can be understood only once Holmes's text is placed in the context of Monk's much earlier *Awful Disclosures* and the subsequent nativist rhetoric it generated. And so, even though Monk's narrative and her subsequent public oratory contributed directly to the regressive politics of religious intolerance and ethnocentrism burgeoning in antebellum America, her ground-breaking depictions of the female bodies trapped behind convent walls and their painfully stifled voices broaden our understanding of the political as well as literary power that American women wielded throughout the nineteenth century.

4

Southern Oratory and the Slavery Debate in Caroline Lee Hentz's *The Planter's Northern Bride* and Harriet Jacobs's *Incidents in the Life of a Slave Girl*

"It is doubtful if there ever has been a society in which the orator counted for more than he did in the Cotton Kingdom," observed historian William Garrott Brown in his 1903 cultural history, *The Lower South in American History*.[1] Permeating all sectors of antebellum southern culture, this oral tradition, according to southern historians and commentators, produced a passion for rhetoric that effectively impeded the production of a distinctly southern literature. Because of an "intense desire to master the spoken word," early-twentieth-century historian Virginius Dabney concludes, "the cherished ambition of almost every young Southerner was for a public rather than a literary career."[2] Nineteenth-century southern novelist William Gilmore Simms concurs, attributing southerners' inability to "produce a national literature" to the fact that they are a "purely agricultural people" and therefore tend to produce "great orators" instead.[3] Yet in this chapter I show that the southern oratory that flourished over the forty-year period preceding the Civil War, rather than impeding the development of a southern literary tradition, in fact shaped southern women's pro-slavery and abolitionist writings. While in the preceding chapter I illustrated how Monk draws upon general interest in the female voice and nativist anxieties about immigrants' impact on it to produce anti-Catholic sentiment, in the following pages I will show how writers contribute to the slavery question by focusing their narratives on the southern oral tradition and its effect on both the female voice and women's public speech. Though on opposite sides of the slavery debate, both

Caroline Lee Hentz, in her pro-slavery response to *Uncle Tom's Cabin, The Planter's Northern Bride* (1854), and Harriet Jacobs, in her auto-biographical narrative of slavery, *Incidents in the Life of a Slave Girl* (1861), place the southern oratory that matured in response to increasing antislavery feeling at the center of the southern worlds they create. More specifically, both writers depict in dramatically different ways the impact that southern oratory has on the female voice and strictures against women's public speech in order to persuade readers of their political positions. While Hentz shows how a white woman's "correct" voice and public speech restore order to a plantation owner's oratory and thus to his slave community, Jacobs depicts in detail the slave woman's unique relation to both southern men's oratory and its codes for woman's language. Numerous scholars have recently noted the persistent interest of Jacobs's narrative in women's relation to words, speech, and silence.[4] Yet none have placed Jacobs's tropes within the context of the oratorical tradition in which her narrative is embedded. Thus, once we read the two texts in light of antebellum accounts of southern oratorical practice, we can see the extent to which both writers' literary productions rely upon, and Jacobs's finally critiques, southern oratorical culture and women's place within it.

"Fiery, Voluptuous, Indolent": Southern Oratory

As early as 1785 Thomas Jefferson described reigning perceptions regarding regional differences in the United States: "In the North they are cool, sober, laborious, [and] persevering, [while] in the South they are fiery, voluptuous, indolent, [and] unsteady."[5] These regional distinctions, according to numerous contemporary language theorists, in turn determined the kind of English that Americans spoke. Charlestonian Reverend Best argues in his *Dissertation upon Oratory* (1800) that American English as it is spoken in the North "has little or no inflexion" because of the "rugged harshness" of its speakers' elocution.[6] The "asperity of sound and roughness of tone [which] predominate" are, according to Best, "injurious to melody" and "repugnant to delicacy" (47–9). "Destitute of . . .

77

smoothness and harmony" (47), American English, particularly as it is spoken in the North, is reduced to "a jargon of various tongues," according to Maria McIntosh in *Woman in America: Her Work and Her Reward* (1850).[7] Though numerous language commentators, as I illustrated in the first chapter, claim that this harsh tone is character-istic of American elocution at its best, southern writers on American English argue that Americans need "to cultivate 'Melody of Lan-guage' " (Best, 44) in order to produce a more aesthetically compel-ling speech. Rather than inhibiting political oratory as northern linguists contend, this pleasing speech is even more rhetorically and politically persuasive than the existing rhetorical style because, according to Best, "various intonations of the voice" are needed to "irresistibly seize the hearers, and lead the passions captive" (79).

Directly reflecting the "voluptuous" and "fiery" character of the region, southern oratory in the antebellum period became distinc-tive and rhetorically powerful because of its implementation of this melodic speech.[8] Unlike women, whose public speech, as I showed in the first chapter, is impeded by the tone of their voices, the sound of these men's public speech enhances its content. Because the southern orator could not, according to Garrott Brown, "touch the artistic sense of the [southern] people with pictures or statues or verses or plays," "the man who wished to lead or to teach must be able to speak"; in short "he must charm [his audience] with [his] voice" (127). Fortunately, southern life prepared the aspiring orator for his task. In his *Literature of the South* (1910), Montrose Moses claims that it is the extravagance of plantation life that produces the "expansiveness of expression . . . [and] plethora of high-sounding phrases, colored by excess of feeling"[9] that typify southern oratory. The antebellum southern orator, according to George Wauchope, is "almost histrionic, stately, . . . excessively dignified, [and] fervidly eloquent."[10] According to Charles Kent, he speaks his mind "in the richest tones of forensic eloquence . . . with a freedom approaching volubility and a [great] love of ornamentation."[11] This orator uses what Thomas Watson describes in *History of Southern Oratory* (1909) as a "well modulated voice . . . [full of] charm and a sense of melody" to produce a "flamboyant, ornate . . . type of oratory" characterized by "copious floridity" and "unspeakable . . . exalted passion."[12]

The southern orator's inherently more melodic and embellished speech produces profoundly powerful reactions in his listening audience. In *Sterling's Southern Orator* (1866), for example, Richard Sterling describes the orator's "big manly voice" as "by turns patient and indignant, bold or yielding, as it suits his purpose."[13] Alternately "exhort[ing], threaten[ing], supplicat[ing], [and] persuad[ing]," this paradigmatic orator successfully compels his listeners to "hang breathless on his lips [and] . . . to follow him in all his windings, through every change of feeling and passion" as "he lashes his opponents with his satire; withers them with his scorn; [and] annihilates them with his terrible, his resistless powers" (42). Because the southern orator, according to Garrott Brown, is not concerned with "meeting the requirements of any standard of public speech," but rather with "rousing, convincing, [and] overwhelming the men in front of him," his "sentences sometimes rush like charging cavalry," his phrases "ring out like bugle calls," and in general his language reflects his "passionate purpose" (148). In *A Southern Speaker* (1856) D. Barton Ross theorizes about the reasons for the southern orator's profound impact on listeners. The speaker's combination of "logic with eloquence and emotion" is designed to inspire his audience "with noble and generous passions" because "the great truths . . . are taught to us" not by reason alone but also "by our instincts, our sentiments . . . and our passions."[14] Fifty years earlier, Reverend Best had argued that it is only when "sublime truths" are "accompanied with animated delivery" that "the moving fibres are shaken, the soul is moved, and . . . we feel ourselves *changed, converted, regenerated*" (80). The orator who perhaps most successfully "converted" southerners to his political views was Jefferson Davis. Speaking "with an even tuneful flow of words . . . the lowest notes of which . . . rose as a sound of a trumpet," according to Thomas Watson, Davis was able "to convey the strongest emotions," filling the "hearts of his hearers with [an] unspeakable passion" (55–6) to protect the geopolitical autonomy of the South.

Devoted to intensifying regional pride and identity, southern oratory played a crucial role in southerners' increasingly passionate verbal and finally physical defense of slavery as a social institution. Claiming that "oratory . . . is the instrument of freedom" (14) and "eloquence is the satellite of liberty" (24), Reverend Best, at the turn into the nineteenth century, calls for all white southern "men of abilities . . . to cultivate oratory" (29) as a means of ensuring the continued autonomy of the South. And southern oratory did in fact flourish as southern identity was challenged. As "the voice of the Old South increased in volume" (Moses, 195), the characteristic emotionalism of southern oratory also became, according to Watson, "more acute, concentrated, and impassioned" (37). This heightened emotion combined with "the greatness of the political issues" to make the antebellum era "the period of exceptionally great oratory – the greatest era of the spoken word in all constitutional history" (30, 35). Yet, rather than ensuring liberty for white southerners as Best contends, the speech of pro-slavery advocates carried the South into a war that resulted in the abolition of the slave system upon which white cultural identity had come increasingly to depend. Admitting that southerners "were wrought up, by passionate appeals, to fight out a question which in every other country was adjusted [to] without the loss of a single human life," Watson concludes that southern orators singlehandedly "plunged us into the War of Secession" (88).

This politically powerful oratory determined not only the future of southern culture but the role that women and more particularly their speech played within it. In her landmark study of nineteenth-century southern womanhood, *The Southern Lady* (1970), Anne Firor Scott points out that "the image of the lady took deep root" in the South with "far-reaching social consequences."[15] While descriptions of the southern "girl" are as diverse as they are plentiful, commentators unanimously agree that the quality of her voice and the diffidence of her speech must be irreproachable. While George Fitzhugh describes the southern girl as "nervous, fickle, capricious, delicate, diffident, and dependent" in his 1854 *Sociology for the South*,[16] Thomas Nelson Page claims, in his retrospective *Social Life in Old Virginia* (1897), that she is "delicate, dainty, mischievous,

tender, God-fearing, [and] inexplicable."[17] In 1863 correspondence, the novelist Augusta J. Evans agrees that the southern girl is
"graceful, pretty, witty and pleasant," but she also describes the
southern girl's "scanty" information, "defective" judgment,
"dwarfed" reasoning faculties, and "weak and frivolous" aspira-
tions.[18] Though much thought is devoted to her physical and intellectual characteristics, Evans and others place greater stress on the
southern girl's voice and speech. Unlike the "strong-minded women
of the North," who southerners depict as having "the stern character
of the lecturer upon the rostrum," the southern woman, as Henry
Jackson describes her in *The Southern Women of the Second American
Revolution* (1863), is characterized by "soft words of friendship whis-
pered into the ear of [the] lonely and forlorn."[19] The southern
woman's goal, according to Maria McIntosh in *Woman in America*
(1850), is to produce a "nicely modulated voice, whose subtle melody steals sometimes to the heart wrapped in . . . selfishness" (84).
The "delicious, low, slow, musical speech" (56) that Thomas Nelson
Page describes as characteristic of the southern woman's voice enables her to "lay the bed rock foundation of innate virtue" with
which to "calm the unruly passion of sons and husbands" (74).
Because "the celestial music" of the southern "woman's soothing
voice" is able to "speak those sweet words of comfort" (17), Henry
Jackson concludes, in *Southern Women of the Second American Revolution,* that it follows that she must dutifully use "her gentle voice"
to produce "cheerful conversation" that makes the southern man
forget all "disagreeable subjects" (22). Thus, by claiming that cacophonous voices and disorderly public speech are an exclusive
feature of northern women, these social commentators heighten the
impact of their theories on southern women, who subsequently
come to believe that their speech upholds and protects southern
identity.

These commentaries effectively ensure that southern women remain the subject rather than the speakers of southern oratory.[20]
Posed against the "impudent clique of unsexed females" in the
North, who, in the imaginations of southern men, take to "the
platforms of public debate and enter into all the rough and tumble

of the war of words," southern women are applauded, by John Cocke in an 1853 letter, for their refusal to engage in any speech, public or private, that challenges the highly patriarchal structure of southern society.[21] According to Maria McIntosh, the southern woman should exercise "her influence, not by public associations, and debates, and petitions, but in the manifestation of all feminine grace," and in so doing "soften by her influence" both "master" and "slave" (118–19). In order to remind southern women readers of the unseemliness of women's public speech, McIntosh describes a fictitious northern woman, Flirtilla, who "talks and laughs very loudly at all public places, lectures, concerts . . . and has sometimes, even in the house of God, expressed audibly her assent with or dissent from the preacher" (74). Even after the war, Captain J. M. Taylor compliments southern ladies, in an 1868 speech, for not enraging "the delicate retirement of their sex, by an open and active participation in the political issues of the day."[22]

The silence that characterizes the southern woman in public extends to and shapes her private speech as well. Even in the private sphere "a woman ought not to speak what she pleased," Robert Charlton told the 1853 graduates of La Grange Female College, because a woman's husband was responsible for her language.[23] In an 1828 correspondence, Judge John H. Bryan sought to control legally women's private as well as public speech by passing a law to punish "a woman who abuses her husband to strangers" by having "her tongue cut out, or slit at least."[24] Such attitudes pressured southern women to stifle their speech in private as well as in public. Newly married, Anne Beale Davis vowed in her diary never to offend with her "tongue" but, in language reminiscent of Monk's narrative, to "hold it in with bit and bridle and speak charitably of all persons."[25] In *Recollections of a Southern Matron* (1839), Caroline Gilman tells all American women who want "domestic happiness" that they must learn "to repress a harsh answer, to confess a fault, and to stop (right or wrong) in the midst of self-defence."[26] "A good wife," she concludes, must speak in "tones of cheerfulness [even] when her frame is drooping" (257).

With her strict control over the sound of her voice as well as the content of her public and private speech, the prototypical southern woman epitomized for southerners the social benefits of the slave system. Elevated by slavery, as Thomas Dew argues in his 1835 defense of it, from a position of servitude as a "mere *beast of burthen* ... the slave of men" to "the equal and the idol" of man, "the cheering and animating centre of the family circle,"[27] the southern woman represents the social improvements the slave system brings to the South.[28] With the increase in leisure that slavery afforded, the southern woman, by suppressing her "most violent feelings" and "curb[ing] her most ardent desires" – in short, by refusing to "give *utterance* to her passions and emotions like a man"[29] – suddenly had the ability to transform herself, according to Dew, from a "licentious" female who indulges in "the feverish joys of a dissipated hour" into a "pure and simple" icon of "domestic life" (*Pro-Slavery*, 445).

However, opposed as the social conditions of white women and slaves are in antebellum southern rhetoric, many commentators continue to point out the similarities between the two groups. In 1850 South Carolina planter James Hammond, for example, expresses disdain for both, reflecting in his diary that women, like slaves, are "mostly fools and savages and not to be called either civilized or thinking or reasonable Beings."[30] In light of Hammond's statement, Mary Chesnut's famous but controversial comment that "all married women ... and girls who live on in their fathers' houses are slaves" gains force.[31] According to Chesnut, it is because "women sell themselves and are sold in marriage" that "all married women" end up "slaves" (729). Reverend Frederick Ross concurs, in his 1857 *Slavery Ordained of God*, that "God has placed master and slave in the same relation as husband and wife."[32] In 1845 a writer to the *North Carolina Standard* who identifies himself only with his initials argues more specifically that the similarity in the status of free women and slaves occurs because there is "no essential difference between the legal condition of the married woman and that of the slave."[33] In its commentary on the article, the *North Carolina Standard* agrees that it is an "undeniable fact, that the wives of Christian husbands are as much slaves, so far as privation of rights is concerned, as the negroes of the utmost South." "The parallel," it concludes, "between what the slave *is* and what the wife *might be,* is both striking and complete." Antebellum laws regarding child custody, domestic violence, and cohabitation in turn consistently reflected the similarity in legal status between the two groups. Like slave women, free women had no legal control over the children they bore. Because men had complete custody of their children, the southern woman, be she slave or free, gained the legal right to her offspring only if her husband named her guardian.[34] Men's proprietary rights extended to their wives as well. Until 1857 a husband was legally allowed to beat his wife, provided that the weapon was "not thicker than his little finger," according to the *Raleigh Register* (1825), and the practice was socially accepted long after it was outlawed.[35] When women tried to escape such physical abuse, their husbands ran advertisements for their fugitive wives. Almost as numerous, according to historians, as notices for fugitive slaves and stray horses, these ads included physical descriptions of the runaways and injunctions against harboring or seducing them, as men through 1861 could collect damages for such offenses.[36]

In order to make significant contributions to pro-slavery and abolitionist sentiment, both Caroline Lee Hentz and Harriet Jacobs focus on the interdependencies between these two groups and, more particularly, on the women's language that supposedly distinguishes them. I show that, in *The Planter's Northern Bride,* Caroline Lee Hentz seeks to instill pro-slavery sentiment in her readers by illustrating how the voice and insistent public silence of a "proper" woman restore political authority to a pro-slavery orator whose personal and rhetorical potency have been damaged by the disorderly speech of his first wife. Yet while Hentz depicts free women employing their submissive speech to reinforce the politically powerful pro-slavery language of southern men, Jacobs illustrates how one slave woman effectively resists the abusive language that constitutes her experience of slavery not with the voice of the southern lady, but with speech that publicly challenges her master's entitlement to victimize her sexually. Hentz and Jacobs, then, produce very different political discourses by showing how women use their language to authorize and undermine the rhetoric of southern men. In so

doing they revise, first, the notion that southern oratory has a deleterious effect on the creation of a distinctly southern literary tradition
and, second, the notion that public speech in the antebellum South
was an exclusively male pursuit.

"A Heroine, for All That"

A direct rejoinder to abolitionist writing in general and *Uncle Tom's
Cabin* in particular, *The Planter's Northern Bride* depicts in detail the
protection that plantation life affords slaves, who are represented as
being too ignorant and naive to protect themselves.[37] To make its
point, *The Planter's Northern Bride* tells the story of an upstanding
southern man's quest for a second wife whose impeccable voice and
inhibited public speech will compensate for the indignities he has
suffered at the hands of his former wife. Fleeing the South that has
witnessed his wife's adultery and desertion, Mr. Moreland heads
North and finds in a village church choir a young woman whose
pure voice testifies to her irreproachable and stereotypical femininity. After marrying Eulalia, Moreland returns with his new wife to his
broken home and disorderly plantation. Eulalia, through the heal-
ing powers of her voice and example, restores order to both. In so
doing, she enables her once-inarticulate husband to succeed in
public oratory, and the novel closes with Moreland convincing his
slaves that they do indeed desire enslavement. However, while the
novel tracks the socially redemptive power of the traditional female
voice, it begins with an account of the destruction that a woman's
disorderly speech wreaks on a slave-owning community.

In Hentz's text, Claudia Moreland challenges the reigning assumptions of the plantation life over which she presides by describing passions that Thomas Dew and other southern thinkers claim
proper southern women, because of the "civilizing" effect of slavery,
no longer experience. Trained as a child in Europe for "public
exhibition in the song and the dance" (373), Claudia learns early
how to produce "wild, passionate bursts of harmony" (367), which
continue to set her apart from the community of southern women
she attempts to join by marrying the affluent planter Mr. Moreland.

Once on Moreland's plantation, Claudia refuses to submit to the vocal and by extension sexual control that slave-owning men exert over southern women. The disorder among Claudia's musical instruments is matched by the unruliness of her voice. The "harp with broken strings," the "guitar in the same neglected plight," and "a piano with uncovered keys, and burdened with music books" (314) correspond to the disorderly tone of voice in which Claudia speaks about the "dark passions" (323) she feels, first for Moreland and then, when he fails to satisfy her, for other men. Blaming himself for "yielding to the impulse of passion" (462) that Claudia provoked in him, Moreland tries to regain control over his marriage by redirecting his own and Claudia's energy into slaveholding and the acquisition of "more land." But Claudia responds to this manipulative strategy with a critique of the slave system to which her social freedom and desires have been sacrificed. Claudia recognizes the similarities between her husband's tyrannical treatment of herself and his slaves, and so tells Moreland that he is a master and tyrant who wants her "to cringe to his will, like the slaves in the kitchen" (366). Hoping to safeguard his dwindling authority, Moreland contends that his wife is more "a slave" to "her own wild passions" (344) than to him. Though admitting that a woman "without impulse or passion ... may wear the yoke without feeling it" (366), Claudia finally decides to reject Moreland's authority and leaves him for another man.

Abandoned by a "corrupt" woman who refuses to accept southern codes for women's behavior and speech, Moreland goes North to find a wife whose voice reflects the kind of control that can restore his authority on the plantation. Imagining that "the hearts of people" become increasingly "cold" the farther they live "from the burning sun of the tropics, and that passion, the great central fire of the human bosom, [is] ... wanting in the less genial latitude" (60) of the North, Moreland goes to church and listens to the choir, hoping to find "among the voices" one that meets his needs (34). One voice, that of Eulalia, seems to Moreland "to drown every other" as, "sweet and soft and feminine beyond expression," it rises above the rest "like the imagined hymn of an angel, clear and swelling" (34). Overpowered by Eulalia's remarkably pure voice, which keeps "rolling and warbling round the arching walls of the church, till the house [i]s filled with their melody," Moreland begins to imagine it as "something visible, as well as audible" (35). "Surrounded by a halo of music and prayer" (61), Eulalia seems to him to be pure enough to control not only his passions but her own as well. As Eulalia and Moreland sing together, her "seraph voice" with its "warm, pure breath float[s] against his glowing cheek" (69) and triggers for Moreland the memory "of a voice which had in other hours enthralled his soul; – but that had breathed of the passions of earth" (45). However, the "purity and bloom" (36) that continue to distinguish Eulalia's voice from Claudia's convince him that even "in the wildest paroxysm of anger, [her] voice would soothe [him] into peace" (307).

Eulalia's voice continues to distinguish her from Claudia after Moreland and Eulalia marry. The "pure, sweet, fresh womanliness, a virgin delicacy" and "deep, genuine, but unobtrusive piety" that Eulalia possesses equip her, in Moreland's mind, with "every qualification wanting in the brilliant, but misguided Claudia" (101). While "not so dazzlingly white as Claudia's snowy, but perjured hand," Eulalia's hands remain attractively "pure from the stains of labour" (64) that signify northern rural life. Though Eulalia's "simple travelling dress" as well as her hands bear "little resemblance to the brilliant and magnificently decorated being who had once before clasped Moreland's plighted hand," her marriage vows, unlike Claudia's, are "pure and holy" (175). Even after marriage, Eulalia's "meek, depreciating [sic] speech" seems to Moreland a model of "truth, simplicity, guilelessness, and purity" impossible for the "fashionable belle" (157). Likewise, despite the birth of a child, Eulalia retains the "child-like, virgin innocence" that reminds Moreland of her days as "a vestal in the white-robed village choir" (422). "Grave, serene, and holy, [with a] youthful purity," Eulalia is able to preserve in Moreland a love that, unlike his passion for the "transgressing Eve" (365), "can never change" (106). Yet while the women's differences are profound – "evil passions" darkening "the brilliant face of the one" and "purity, goodness, truth, and love" imparting "to the other an almost celestial charm" (363) – it is their voices – the "divine sweetness of [Eulalia's] voice" as opposed to Claudia's "impassioned gestures" and language (377) – that signal most clearly the differences between them.

Through her voice, Eulalia not only differentiates herself from Moreland's sexually unruly former wife, but also inculcates in Claudia's daughter, Effie, the southern femininity on which Moreland's peace of mind and power depend. Though Effie has inherited the "passionate and wilful temper" of her mother, "heaven" intervenes, placing "her in Eulalia's keeping" (377). In order to neutralize "the curse" of vocal and sexual rebellion that has been "transmitted" to Effie from her biological mother, Eulalia must teach Effie how to speak properly. Fluctuating between passionate outbursts and language "vulgarized by African phrases, learned by constant association with the negroes," Effie is a "little wilful being, whose childish prattle" (479) reflects Claudia's influence as well as her maternal disinterest. A writer for the *Hillsborough Recorder* in 1825 encourages the southern mother not to trust her child with any caretaker exhibiting improper maternal sentiment, because the child "may . . . learn to lisp vulgarity and obscenity" and might acquire "a pronunciation and accent, such as may never be fully corrected."[38] In *Northwood* (1852) Sarah J. Hale similarly warns that a slave "allowed to go on in his own idiomatic jargon" will "vulgarize and render disgusting" the speech of "Southern ladies" whose "manner of speech and intonation" subsequently sounds "so '*niggerish*' as to become unintelligible to those unversed in that peculiar dialect."[39] Though Effie's elocution has been doubly "damaged" by her mother's and the servants' influences, Moreland asks Eulalia to "make her like yourself . . . all that is lovely and good" (217). If she succeeds, he will reward Eulalia by forgetting that Effie "ever had another mother" (217). To displace Claudia and exert her own maternal influence, Eulalia appropriates the piano that epitomizes Claudia's behavioral and vocal dissonance. Whenever Effie resists her authority, Eulalia subdues "her into the gentlest obedience, by singing a few simple strains" (307) at the piano. Admitting that she is "a good girl, when mamma sings" (307), Effie is gradually convinced by the sound of Eulalia's voice to replace Claudia's "coarse, violent language" with Eulalia's "angelic sweetness" (465). Continually reminded by Eulalia not to say, "I won't" (310), Effie of her own accord finally "*says gently* 'I had rather not,' " and transfixes Moreland with her "transformation from passion to gentleness" (311).

Only after traditional southern femininity, as reflected in women's control over their voices and passionate speech, is restored can Moreland overwhelm his abolitionist opponents with the oratorical skills that define southern manhood. Like all traditional southern orators, Moreland has "an exceedingly clear, sweet, and finely modulated voice" that swells "like a well-tuned melodious instrument" in order to "charm the ear" (87). Yet his rhetorical skills fail to persuade his northern listeners of his pro-slavery arguments. Though he "defie[s] all the eloquence of the North to induce" the slave with whom he travels to escape (15), Moreland cannot convince his audiences that the "clanking chains of which [abolitionists] speak are mere figures of speech" and that one hears slaves' "voices singing in the fields of labor" (51) rather than screaming in pain. Because Eulalia wants her abolitionist father "to hear him talk, and [to] listen to his eloquent self-defense" (56), Mr. Hastings finally "throws down the gauntlet" of politics while conversing with Eulalia's suitor. Yet the "fine and flattering speech" that impresses Eulalia sounds to her father "very much like one prepared and polished for the occasion" (63). In comparison with the "thick and incoherent" (87) rhetorical style that characterizes Mr. Hastings's "yankee" speech, Moreland's "lofty tone" and "high words" (107) fail to impress and then finally offend Mr. Hastings.

Yet, once Moreland's oratory is empowered by his wife's "seraphic voice" which with its "tone of more than mortal sweetness" (348) influences the slaves as well as Effie, he is able to quell the abolitionist "eloquence" (496) that sways his slaves. Accepting into his home the itinerant northern preacher Brainard, Moreland is initially impressed by the preacher's "voice of rare and winning power" (459). Because the planter is at first unaware of the preacher's politics, Brainard is free to orchestrate insurrection among the slaves by speaking "burning words" to them in his "low, sweet-toned voice"

(456). "Gifted with an eloquence passing that of the sons of men," Brainard wraps "his influence" (489) around the slaves in order "to gratify his own unhallowed passions" (458) and almost succeeds in causing a rebellion before Moreland intervenes. While her voice has revitalized Moreland's oratory, Eulalia does not attempt to add her own speech to her husband's public articulations. Instead, she remains so far removed from the public arena that, though a spectator, she cannot "hear one syllable of what was uttered" (508). His authority thus unequivocally reasserted, Moreland employs all the skills of southern oratory to convince his slaves that they desire servitude. "His voice deepening into sternness and his eye kindling with indignation" (500), Moreland articulates his pro-slavery arguments with "indescribable emotion" (502). "Looking earnestly in his face, and drinking in his words with countenances expressive of shame, remorse, and returning devotion" (502), the slaves are finally moved by their master's arguments to prostrate themselves before him. Reduced to "entreating for pardon, and imploring with tears and sobs not to be sent away from him" (505), Moreland's slave audience finally testifies to the effectiveness of his oratorical skills and to the important role the female voice and women's public silence plays in upholding it.

"Stinging, Scorching Words"

While in Caroline Lee Hentz's conservative text, women's voices and their public silence uphold southern men's oratory and thus the slave system it champions, Harriet Jacobs focuses, in her critique of slavery, on the slave woman's unique relation to both the sound and substance of southern women's language. In *Incidents in the Life of a Slave Girl,* slave women's stifled speech and their defenselessness against men's talk are central to their experience of oppression.[40] Jacobs depicts women's experience of slavery as one of continual verbal assault and points out that it is slaves' public silence that perpetuates their oppression. Though most slaves are effectively held captive by the public language that, as we saw in Moreland's final speech, continually reminds slaves of their inferiority, Jacobs describes how one woman learns to speak back, not with the appealing voice of the southern lady, but with language that publicly challenges the southern oratory that dehumanizes the black men and women who form its subject. Indeed, it is "by the talk" (6) that surrounds and infiltrates her first home that Jacobs's autobiographical heroine, Linda Brent, first learns that she is a slave, but she realizes the extent of her servitude only after she enters her master's home and hears his speech. When Linda turns fifteen, Mr. Flint begins "to whisper foul words in [her] ear" and to crowd her "young mind with unclean images, such as only a vile monster could think of" (27). Unlike the passionate oratory that convinces Moreland's slaves of his moral superiority, the "stinging, scorching words" with which Flint tells Linda that she has been "made for his use, made to obey his command in *every* thing" because she is "nothing but a slave" burn her "ear and brain like fire" (18), strengthening her resolve to resist his authority. Forced to "listen to such language as he [sees] fit to address" to her (32), Linda finds herself in the common situation of "the slave girl" who is victimized by "the foul talk of her master and his sons" (51).[41] The sexually lurid speech that passes from one generation of southern men to the next ensures that Flint's male relatives will pour "vile language into the ears" of Linda's "innocent . . . child" (179) as well. Yet, by depicting as sexually corrupt southern men's pro-slavery language, Jacobs calls the rhetorical power of their political program into question.

Although southern men in Jacobs's account use their speech not, as Hentz contends, to maintain an orderly and equitable slave community but to victimize slave women, it is the silence these men demand from their slaves about their abuse that constitutes their greatest violation of human rights. Swearing to kill her if she is "not as silent as the grave" (28), Mr. Flint depends on Linda's public silence to conceal his wrongdoing. However, his sexual tyranny also requires the silence of the larger community of slaves. Like the nuns in Monk's narrative, Flint's slaves do not dare "to ask the cause" of the women's screams they hear, because they are "aware that to speak" of "the guilty practices" that occur in Flint's house is "an offense that never [goes] unpunished" (28). Momentarily forgetting that it is "a crime for a slave to tell who [is] the father of her child" (13), one of Flint's slaves reveals their sexual relations. To check her vocal indiscretion, her master promptly reinforces her lack of physical freedom by selling her and their children, an act he justifies by telling her, "You have let your tongue run too far; damn you!" (13). With such examples before them, slave mothers do not "dare to tell who [is] the father of their children . . . except in whispers among themselves" (35). Aware that a slave's "free" speech occurs only under the compulsion of the whipping post, Flint, like many slave owners, refuses to whip the women he rapes, fearing that "the application of the lash" might lead inadvertently "to remarks that would . . . expose him" (35) to the public.

Southern men exert tyrannical control over their slaves' speech not only to silence their accounts of abuse but also to squelch their discussions about general slave conditions. These men determine the content of public narratives of slave life not only with their own public speech, but also by controlling who engages in public debate. Only rarely are slaves "bold enough to utter [abolitionist] sentiments to their masters" in response to "the enormous lies" the masters "tell their slaves" (43) about the quality of their life compared with life in the North. By overpowering their slaves' accounts of their condition with pro-slavery rhetoric, masters keep the slaves from objecting to the atrocities committed on the plantations. Central to her description of the terrible "cruelties" (46) that occur under one master's rule is Jacobs's focus on the terrified and complicitous silence that the slaves are forced to maintain. The murders that this master commits "pass without comment" among the slaves, "no words [are] used" to describe the tortures he inflicts, and in general "nothing [is] said" (47) about his sadism. Because any slave who voices even the mildest criticism is beaten "for telling lies about white men" (64), "slaves dar[e] not tell" any visiting northerner the truth, even "if he ha[s] asked them" (74). Though slaveholders, including Flint, often join the church and publicly mouth religious doctrine in order to "end all the damned slang" (74) about their abuse of power, Flint's conversation at least, once he is alone with his slaves, gives "no indication that he ha[s] 'renounced the devil and all his works' " (74). Hearing only the master's side of the slavery story, rhetorically enhanced by religious overtones, the visiting northerner thus "suppresses every thought and feeling at variance" with slavery (44) and becomes a pro-slavery advocate.

Though slaves are compelled to remain silent, Jacobs cannot understand why the "free men and women" who make up her reading audience allow their own "tongues [to] falter in maintenance of the right" (29–30). Rather than entertaining themselves by listening to the southern orator or "the thrilling voice of Jenny Lind in Metropolitan Hall," northern audiences, according to Jacobs, should listen to "the thrilling voices of poor hunted colored people" that go "up, in an agony of supplication" (191). Once they do so, they will be forced to tell "American slaveholders" that "it is wrong to traffic in men" (73), and then they will see how superficial southern oratorical strategies really are.

As a central part of her critique, Jacobs reveals that the voices of southern women are not protected by slavery, as commentators claim, but in fact are adversely affected by it. According to Jacobs, free white women as well as slave women suffer because of the sexual excess that characterizes southern men's speech. However, unlike slave women, southern ladies can fight back with an unseemly language that unfortunately only reinforces slavery's atrocities. Like the slaves who wait on them, southern "girls" also learn, by overhearing "such talk as should never meet youthful ears" (52), about the illicit sexual practices in which southern men indulge. It is because he has "no regard [for] his marriage vows" (36) that the slaveholder uses his speech to seduce and even to compel slave women into having sexual relations with him. Yet the stress that these extramarital activities exert on southern wives finds expression chiefly in their inability to maintain the strict control over the tone and content of their speech that McIntosh and others encourage. Susceptible to "violent outbreaks of jealous passion" (28), Mrs. Flint, for example, cannot control the sound or substance of her speech in the home. Though she tries to speak "kindly" to Linda, she increasingly loses "control over her passions" (34) and yells at her. Weeping and "sometimes groan[ing]," she speaks about her husband's inconstancy "in tones so sad" (33) that Linda pities her. Yet, while Linda admits that "one word of kindness from her would have brought me to her feet" (32), Mrs. Flint instead launches a verbal attack so offensive that, according to Linda, "no terms were too vile for her to bestow upon me" (32). Not content with verbally assaulting Linda during the day, Mrs. Flint mimics her husband's words to Linda at night. Approaching Linda's bed as she sleeps, Mrs. Flint, according to Linda, "whisper[s] in my ear, as though it was her husband" and then listens "to hear what I would answer" (34). While justifying her actions by accusing Linda of "talking in [her] sleep" (34), Mrs. Flint hopes to discover, in an unconscious exchange of words, the sexual details of Linda's relationship with Flint.

Within this world of abusive language and enforced public silence, Jacobs tracks Linda's gradual acquisition of language that is powerful enough to frustrate and finally free her from her master. Confronted with his sexually abusive language, Linda learns to counter, with her own sexually explicit speech, the slave-owning man's aggression. Even as a child Linda discusses the condition of slaves with her Uncle Ben; and once Ben becomes a man, he actively resists slavery with his speech. Refusing to "seal" his "lips," he talks, sings, and laughs when he pleases, incurring the wrath of his owner. When, with a "firm set mouth," Ben finally tells his family that he is running away to avoid being incarcerated for his rebellious speech, his mother "shudder[s] at" the subversive strength of "his words" (22). With Ben's radical speech as a model, Linda tries to use her own speech to fend off the oppression that inevitably changes "slave girls' laughter [into] . . . sighs" (29). Not resembling in sound or content the language that typifies the southern lady, this new slave woman's speech insistently asserts that women have complex sexual lives and that they have an indisputable right to choose their partners in them. Linda thus repeatedly refuses to comply with Flint's sexual demands, proclaiming her sexual if not legal independence from him. Unperturbed by Mr. Flint's threat to "cowhide" her if she speaks to the man she loves, Linda publicly encourages her fiancé to go "where his tongue would not be tied" (42). After causing Flint's voice to become "hoarse with rage" (75) as he witnesses her publicly defiant speech, Linda further frustrates Flint's attempts to seduce her by choosing a lover who is remarkable for the atypical sensitivity of his language. When the affluent landowner Mr. Sands first approaches Linda, she is surprised to find that she does not "trembl[e] within hearing of his voice" (55). "An eloquent gentle-man" (54) who speaks "kind and encouraging words" (58) not only to her but to her whole family, Mr. Sands impresses Linda because of his difference from Flint. "Encouraged by his kind words" (54), she accepts him as a lover and thereby foils Flint's attempts to control her sexual life and the vocal interchanges that motivate and occur within it.

Though her affair with Mr. Sands thwarts Flint's plans, it also transforms the way in which Linda speaks. Having resolved to "be virtuous, though . . . a slave" (56), she discovers that by discussing her sexual activity she alters her vocal authority. When she attempts to "utter the dreaded words" of her affair and pregnancy in a "confession" to her grandmother, "the words" stick in her "throat" (56). Initially, her admission to Flint silences him, and he leaves her "house without a word" (56). Although she has preempted his sex-ual advances by choosing a white man who can protect her from Flint's physical abuse, she cannot stop his vocal assaults. Admitting that "I no longer had the power of answering him as I had formerly done" (81), Linda "resolve[s] to bear Flint's abuse in silence" (58). That verbal abuse increases as her pregnancy becomes more pro-nounced. Responsible for her prenatal care, Flint visits Linda and inflicts on her "talk such as would have made the most shameless blush" (59). Though "humiliated" by "such language," Linda feels "too feeble to dispute with him" (61). Repeatedly "subjected to such insults as no pen can describe" (77) in the past, Linda must now, with "words choked in [her] throat" (100), listen silently while Flint "utter[s] oaths terrible enough to palsy a man's tongue" and heaps "every vile epithet he [can] think of" (77) on Linda and her child.

However, Linda learns to use her momentary speechlessness – indeed she amplifies it by hiding in the garret of her grandmother's house – to ensure her own and her children's escape from the institution that denies them a voice. While hiding, Linda overhears a number of "conversations not intended to meet [her] ears" (117) from which she gleans important information. The most sustaining and frustrating aspect of her "silent days . . . in [the] dreary den" (165) lies, according to Linda, in seeing her "children's faces, and [hearing] their sweet voices" without being able "to say, 'Your mother is here'" (148). Though she gets solace from the "merry laughter" (115) of her children, she must sit in silence and helplessness while Mr. Flint tries "to coax and bribe [the] children" (117) to tell him something about her escape. When her son is bitten by a dog, she must bite her own lips until they bleed "to keep from crying out" as she listens to his screams (123). Admitting that it is "torture to a mother's heart, to listen . . . and be unable to go" to (123) her children, Linda nevertheless remains silent, temporarily surrendering "the power of speech" (122). Only when she hears that Mr. Sands is moving away does she break her silence. Imagining that she hears the "two little voices" of her children pleading with her "not to let their father depart without striving to make their freedom secure" (125), she speaks to the father of her children through an open window. Though during Linda's exile in the garret "years [have] passed" and they have not spoken, Linda begs Mr. Sands to let her "speak a few words . . . about emancipating my children" (125–6). Having succeeded with Mr. Sands, Linda proceeds to free herself. Imagining that she hears her mother's "voice . . . whispering loving words into my wounded heart" (90) and her father's "voice . . . bidding me not to tarry till I had reached freedom or the grave" (91), she orchestrates her escape and meets her children in the North. Once safely reunited with them, Linda regains the ability to speak openly about slavery. Proclaiming that "hot weather brings out snakes and slaveholders," and admitting that she likes "one class of venomous creatures as little as [she does] the other," she concludes by saying, "what a comfort it is, to be free to *say* so!" (174).

Though they promote divergent political agendas, both Caroline Lee Hentz's and Harriet Jacobs's novels depend upon the oratorical culture that was central to antebellum southern identity and upon the complex, provocative role that women's voices and public speech played in both sustaining and undermining that culture. In *The Planter's Northern Bride*, Hentz tracks the restorative effects of a northern woman's traditional voice and public silence on a slave community that has been damaged by the disorderly speech of one of its new female members. Empowered by the voice and public silence of his northern wife, the slaveholder Moreland recovers his masculine authority and develops the oratorical skills that go with it to become, by the end of the novel, a successful pro-slavery orator. Thus, by advocating for traditional associations between southern femininity and language, Hentz promotes the political content of Moreland's oratory. Conversely, Harriet Jacobs encourages abolitionist sentiment in readers of *Incidents in the Life of a Slave Girl* by describing, first, the oppression that results from the speech of southern men and, second, the way in which a female slave trains herself to use her speech to resist a slaveholder's sexual abuse. Although their divergent accounts of the southern female's voice and speech produce divergent politics, Hentz's and Jacobs's shared interest in the impact of women's voices on the southern oratorical tradition expands our understanding of the mutually dependent relationships between both southern oratory and writing, and women's and men's speech in the antebellum South.

5

Partners in Speech

Reforming Labor, Class, and the Working Woman's Body in Elizabeth Stuart Phelps's *The Silent Partner*

After summarizing the work of "scholars who study the economic, the political, and the realistic novel," Carol Farley-Kessler concludes that Elizabeth Stuart Phelps is "without exception" considered to be "the first American novelist to treat the theme of urban, industrial blight" in her 1871 novel, *The Silent Partner*.[1] Yet literary critics who have recently begun to evaluate the novel's depictions of women labor reformers have argued that the novel is politically conservative, even "regressive." Focusing exclusively on Perley Kelso's quest to develop her voice despite her status as a "silent" partner in the mill, these scholars have argued that, while the book does address the crucial question of how a bourgeois woman can productively use her voice to advocate for mill workers, Perley's public speech ends up reinforcing rather than contesting or subverting the middle-class gender codes that confine her. Pointing out that her public speech champions the mill owners' cause and thereby undermines the workers' will to strike, these analyses conclude that the novel finally "serve[s] the interests of the middle class, registering what is already changed at the sphere boundaries."[2] While Perley's voice and her public speech are indisputably the result of, and so reinforce, her class privilege, I want to expand existing conversations regarding the text's political significance by showing, first, that the political impact of the text does not depend exclusively on the success of a middle-class woman's attempts to exert herself in order to benefit "the hands" of her mill; second, that by focusing on the middle-class woman, rather than on the working women who abound in the text, in order to determine the novel's political contribution, scholars have inadvertently replicated the rhetorical strategies of the bourgeois women who controlled the women's labor reform movement in the 1870s and filtered its politics through a middle-class lens; and third, that by placing the novel within the historical context of the nineteenth-century labor reform movement and its women reformers' descriptions of wage-earning women, we can see how *The Silent Partner* challenges reformers' ideas about such women and their labor rhetoric.

By analyzing *The Silent Partner* in terms of the labor movement to which it contributed we can identify the assumptions structuring the movement's language and the particular ways in which Phelps's fictional text contests those assumptions. In their labor rhetoric, bourgeois reformers consistently equate working women's identity with their own "passionless, innocent, and sexually pure" womanhood in order to highlight the sexual dangers to which these women are susceptible and thereby to promote women's labor reform.[3] Any rare glimpses of sexual divergence among the women they champion only serve to reinforce the political importance that labor reformers ascribe to women's sexual purity. With this middle-class reformatory insistence on sexual uniformity as its point of departure, Phelps's text imagines alternative relations between reformers and the working women they attempt to represent and protect. In *The Silent Partner* it is the woman mill worker Sip Garth, rather than the bourgeois woman, who, with her speech to both Perley and the public, reshapes reformatory paradigms of laborers' sexuality. Inspired by the tortured voices of her co-workers, Sip learns, by listening to Perley's talk, how to reflect through public speech women's negative working conditions and the impact of those conditions on their lives. Thus, Sip's depiction of wage-earning women's differences from middle-class women alters her affluent listener's attitude toward laboring women's consciousness and by extension the labor reform rhetoric that attempts to define and normalize it. Once we analyze mid-nineteenth-century labor reform tracts and more specifically their depictions of wage-earning women, our attention, along with Phelps's, shifts from the affluent silent partner Perley to the working girl Sip and to the other silent partner in the text, her mute sister and companion, Catty. As we refocus not just on the working women but more particularly on their voices and public speech, we can see how *The Silent Partner* attempts to challenge and expand the middle-class attitudes structuring the 1870s women's labor movement and its public language.

"Death or Dishonor"

Because middle-class women imagine wage-earning women's sexuality to be constituted by the same "piety, purity, and submissiveness" (Meyerowitz, 50) that defines their own femininity, their labor reform rhetoric, much like nativist propaganda, makes extensive use of the image of the sexually threatened body of the passionless working woman. In *The Working Girls of Boston* (1889), Carroll Wright asserts the sexual purity of all American women by claiming that "the working girls are as respectable, as moral, and as virtuous as any class of women in our community."[4] Lillie Devereux Blake links the pure working woman's sexual vulnerability to existing labor practices when, in 1883, she tells a congressional committee that "you have to give [women] a respectable means of income or else you are apt to drive them to vice."[5] Labor activists argue that working women's sexual peril is the direct result of limited employment options and women's ensuing poverty. In her popular 1869 labor reform tract, *Think and Act,* Virginia Penny contends that "many [working women] are degraded by their poverty; and their degradation is the cause of nearly all the crime that is committed."[6] As Caroline Dall succinctly states ten years earlier, "The question which is at this moment before the great body of working women is 'death or dishonor': for lust is a better paymaster than the mill-owner."[7] Deprived of other high-paying jobs, at least "one fourth of the lost women of . . . New York [are] driven to the streets and the brothels by destitution" rather than by inclination, according to Penny (99).

Because working women's sexual disorderliness results from repressive labor policy rather than their own unruly desires, both sexual and civic order can be restored, according to middle-class women reformers, by opening labor markets to women. Claiming that "there are very few women that would go astray if honest employments were provided for them at living prices" (23), Penny argues that "the opening of new employments will do much to prevent prostitution" (25). Middle-class reformers' contention that expanding women's access to labor markets and improving their wages would eradicate the sexual unruliness of their passionless but impoverished sisters had little impact on women's working conditions, and so reformers stepped up their campaign by warning that the economic plight of working women threatened the purity not only of women's bodies, but of the national body as well. Because "the social, moral, and intellectual condition of woman has much to do with the honor and standing of a nation," Penny argues that "depravity of the female sex" is "often the first indication of the downfall of a nation" (336.) The resulting impact of working women's sexuality on a female, iconographic America poses a direct threat to the nation. "America . . . goes forth in the freshness of a young and prosperous nation," according to Penny, "but a cancer is consuming her life. Well may she blush for the disgrace that . . . thousands of her women . . . are prostitutes this day from want of remunerative labor" (153).[8]

Activists use the rhetoric of women's sexual endangerment not only to expand workers' access to jobs but to reform the labor in which women are already engaged. Thus, reformers claim that while limited labor opportunities lead working women to prostitution, the work readily available to women also fails to protect their femininity, contributing to their sexual downfall. Dr. G. C. Holland, as cited by Penny, argues that manufacturing girls' "appearance, manners, . . . and moral natures" are the product of their "half-civilized" work conditions. "Constantly associating with ignorant and depraved . . . young persons of the opposite sex," Holland notes that the girls "naturally . . . throw off all restraint in word and act, and become as bad as men" (64). For Caroline Dall the inability of women coal mine workers to distinguish themselves, by clothing or speech, from male miners becomes symptomatic of their oppressive work conditions. Noting that "all are clad in male attire, and oaths that men might shudder to hear issue from lips born to breathe words of sweetness," Dall, like Holland, cites the visible breakdown of workers' femininity as the most extreme by-product of unregulated labor and as the cause of women's "depravity" (47). According to Penny, the strain that "the noisy and exciting labor of a manufactory" exerts on workers' femininity makes women operatives "impulsive" and "often of a desperate and daring character," and finally "brings about [the] dissipation" that ensures their sexual impurity (57).

Reformers warn that the failure of existing labor conditions to reinforce gender differences in the workplace threatens not only women's feminine purity but male workers' masculinity. Noting that "some [work] in which [men] now engage is beneath their dignity as men, and unworthy [of] their strength," Virginia Penny concludes that "a strong healthy man . . . on his knees fitting ladies' shoes . . . is as much out of place, as a woman chopping wood" (25). In her 1863 *Series of Appeals,* Mrs. Nemo argues, "Surely, it is time that men ceased to unman themselves by retailing . . . trinkets and gewgaws, and . . . apply themselves to the ax or the anvil . . . or some calling more worthy [of] their physical endowments."[9] Caroline Dall extends the gendered ideology of separate spheres into the public workplace in order to criticize men's work. Convinced of the appropriate work for each sex, she exclaims, "Fancy a strong man winding silk for a whole day, or sorting colors in floss! How has he ever degraded himself to such girls' work?" (66). Reformers warn that the dissipating effects of "feminine" kinds of commerce on men's masculinity can have physical manifestations. Claiming that "the effeminate manners and habits, and fragile constitutions, in the United States, of young men, arise . . . from the nature of their occupations," Penny demands, "How can they become strong, healthy men, without exercise? . . . Men were made for manly and vigorous pursuits" (289). Focusing on the men who "are employed, by many ladies, to dress their hair," Penny specifies the physical cost of such "effeminate" pursuits by noting "the pale faces, delicate forms, and slender fingers of these men" (290). Mrs. Nemo argues that men "so unmanly as to determine to adhere to their frivolous occupations" should be forced to resemble the women they displace.

"Provided with skirts and shawls, and exquisite little bonnets," these men, Mrs. Nemo is convinced, "with their hairy faces, would doubtless form striking pictures" (20). Thus, by insisting on the gender specificity of certain kinds of work, labor reformers argue that expanding women's employment options will reinforce rather than erode gender differences and result in more manly, healthy men as well as more feminine, pure women.

Although the passionless working woman's purity and the danger that labor poses to it form the cornerstone of reformatory rhetoric, a few labor activists do describe sexual practices among tenement women that conflict with the femininity that reformers depict. Yet, while tenement life and the depravity it imposes on women inhabitants appalls middle-class reformers, their reactions to and accounts of the tenements consistently reveal more about their own sexual attitudes than about wage-earning women's. Helen Campbell, in her 1887 "famous exposé" (Meyerowitz, 66), *The Prisoners of Poverty*, documents, with increasing horror, the different sexual codes that she discovers in workers' tenements. Initially inspired by Penny's reformatory mandate to "save from degradation [her] sisters" (206), Campbell begins a personal campaign in the tenements of New York. Yet, instead of finding pious but impoverished women, Campbell uncovers a den of sexual "foulness" with "dark halls" that she hints "have other uses than as receptacles for refuse and filth."[10] "Hiding behind doors or in corners, or grown bolder, seeking no concealment," the young inhabitants emerge, according to Campbell, only in order to "teach one another such new facts of foulness as may so far have chanced to escape them" (128). According to Campbell, the tenement's sexual "foulness" is inescapable. The "over-crowding, the impossibility of [the] slightest privacy, [and] the constant contact with the grossest side of life" that constitute tenement life "soon . . . destroy every gleam of modesty or decency" and guarantee "sure corruption for every tenant" (234). Prostitution not only fails to repel women raised in these conditions but becomes "merely the final step . . . to the story of ruin and licentiousness that has always existed" for them (235).

In their inevitable interactions with more affluent groups, these women, according to reformers, threaten to infect all sectors of American society with sexual vice. According to Campbell, "The tenement-house stands ... not only as the breeder of disease and physical degeneration for every inmate, but as equally potent in social demoralization for the class who ignore its existence" (235). Because that class hires tenement women as servants, working women's sexuality spills out of the tenement and into the parlor. As Campbell declares, "Hundreds upon hundreds of our domestic servants" come "out of these houses" and "bring inherited and acquired foulness into our homes and lives" (235–6). These women accordingly are held responsible for any sexual vice that occurs in the middle-class families they serve. Because of their sexual background, tenement women "enter a family prepared to meet any advances, and often directly the tempter" (234–5). Campbell imagines these working women's sexuality as a "foul stream" that remains "decorously hidden from view" but that contaminates middle-class sexual purity like a "virus." Because it is "portable," the virus carries a "taint [that] may be discovered even in the remote country" (236). Campbell's anxiety about her own susceptibility to sexual contagion causes her to comment defensively, upon entering the tenement, that even "the most determined [visitor] feels inclined to burn every garment worn during such a quest" (128).

Campbell heightens her readers' awareness of tenement women's more general inferiority in order to reinforce the feminine purity and moral superiority of the middle-class women who control the labor reform movement and model its rhetoric. In her account of tenement women, Campbell stresses the "ignorance and blindness and ... pride, and the many stupidities on which their small lives are founded," offering exhaustive examples to support her opinion (77). Citing women of "all degrees of ignorance and prejudice and stupidity," she nevertheless forces her middle-class audience to "face them, – the ignorant, blind, stupid, incompetent" and to realize that "no count of such indictment alters *our* responsibility toward *them*" (244–5; emphasis added). The final line that she draws between "us" and "them" ensures that the purity of the more powerful class will dominate, despite the threat that tenement women's sexuality poses. Thus, the sexual difference that Campbell highlights finally reinforces the hegemony of the bourgeois purity that defines affluent women activists and so forms the cornerstone of labor reform rhetoric.

However, in the face of evidence of some wage-earning women's disorderly sexuality, reformers intensify their rhetoric by highlighting the significant effect that their voices and public speech have on their wayward, working sisters. Thus they insist on the power of their language to transform even the most resistant, impure women into the fallen but passionless victims they claim working-class women inevitably are. As Penny argues, "The voice [and] the words . . . of refined and amiable women will do much to influence the ignorant or degraded of their own sex" (205). If reformers want "vice and crime . . . to give way to virtue and purity" (204), Penny says, they must be prepared, when "addressing persons of inferior station," to "use simple language, but . . . not fear to put substance in it" (205). With "tongues of fire," pure women have the power to penetrate "the very fibres of [the] hearts" (99) of working women and thus to transform their sexual consciousness.

The success of these transformations is evidenced by working women's voices as well as public speech. In their retrospective public accounts, wage-earning women, according to reformers, use bourgeois models of femininity to describe their sexual depravity and then reinforce those models by depicting their sexual activity as a vocal rather than physical "decline." Acknowledging the rhetorical power of these wage-earning women's accounts, Caroline Dall admits that "if their own words do not touch you, mine . . . will fail" (20). Yet the greater "authenticity" of these accounts, by replicating reformers' assessments of wage-earning women's sexual condition, reinforces bourgeois advocates' labor reform arguments. As one woman, according to Dall, admits, "I was a good girl when I first went to work, and struggled hard to keep pure; but I had not enough to eat" (21). Seeing the errors of their ways, these women, according to labor advocates, couch their own subsequent labor reform rhetoric in the context of middle-class models of femininity. In *Darkness and Daylight* (1895), for example, Helen Campbell describes the public speech of a former prostitute. Her great success is not only the result of "a wonderful gift of language and great natural wit" (241) but "the pathos of her story," which, because of its middle-class appeal, "moved to tears" and held "spellbound" her "vast audiences."[11] However, some wage-earning women, according to reformers, go further – reinforcing models of bourgeois femininity by describing their experiences of sexual activity and harassment as experiences of verbal assault. In *The Working Girls of Boston,* for example, Wright reports that some working girls

> say that the . . . men placed in charge are in the habit of speaking very roughly – . . . they use violent and sometimes bad language before them; others are said to curse and swear at the girls. . . . One girl says she has been subjected to rough words . . . from the foreman . . . other girls speak of the bad language used by employers. (119)

In *The Prisoners of Poverty* Campbell describes one such working girl's gradual sexual "fall" by recounting its altering effect on her speech. Though Rose Haggerty is initially a girl with her "father's quick tongue . . . and scorching word[s]" (22) for those who attempt to assault her purity, her speech and sexuality are transformed by her entry into the workforce. Rose learns the importance of "choking down rash words" and maintaining "silence" in order to survive in an unjust labor market (28). Even these survival strategies eventually fail, and Rose ends up a prostitute. According to Caroline Dall, the workplace has produced countless such "histories of pure, untarnished names" – tales of subsequent sexual abuse told with "dishonored lips" (20).

In *The Silent Partner,* however, Elizabeth Stuart Phelps challenges reformers' confidence in the powerful, transformative effect of their language on sexually rebellious wage-earning women and by extension on the public, by depicting a working woman who insists that work conditions make a difference to all aspects of women's lives. In so doing, Phelps complicates the model of feminine purity upon which, as I have shown, women's labor reform rhetoric is modeled. Motivated by the negative effect of work conditions not only on women's sexual lives but on their ability to speak about them, Sip Garth attempts to represent and defend working women publicly. However, in order to produce the persuasive public language with which the novel closes, she must learn from an affluent woman mill owner how to reshape both the sound and substance of her language. In her exchanges with the middle-class woman, Sip learns how to structure her speech so it can be heard by middle-class audiences, but her "factory-girl's" language in turn transforms her bourgeois listener's perception of her laboring "sisters' " sexuality and her resulting speech about it. In her text, then, Phelps complicates activists' rhetorical reliance on feminine purity by altering the sexual consciousness of the movement's middle-class proponents and by reimagining the movement's new speakers to be wage-earning women who are its central concern.

God's Words – and Catty's

Extrapolating from the concern with women's voices and speech that dominates her text and drives its revisionist politics, Phelps more generally describes the relationship between industry and laborers as a contentious fight for voice. In this struggle, workers' unified speech has a brief but transformative effect on their ability to resist the dehumanizing effects of unregulated labor. Acting as the mouthpiece for the mill owners, the dam that drives the mill "mocks" its workers "with peals of hollow laughter."[12] The work bells, "whose very tongues seem to have stiffened with the cold" (34), control the actions of the mill workers, who "alone are stirring in the dark" because of their "iron voices" (72). Once in operation, the mill literally comes alive, competing with the workers that run it for vitality. The weaving room engines "respire," and, because "with every throb of their huge lungs" they force workers to "swallow their breath" (73), weavers "cough a little [and then] cough a great deal" (75). From coughing fits, the workers "take to swearing roundly" (75) and then to singing. While the mill produces reactive sounds in its workers, it is incapable of containing the effect of their singing. Amid the dirt of the mill, the song emerges "of simple, spotless things" (75) and the "contest between the chorus and the din, . . . the struggle of the melody . . . from loom to loom, . . . from lifted face to lifted face" (76) begins. The machinery becomes a gauge for the momentary shift in power that the song produces, as it "fall[s] into a fit of rage . . . throws its arms about, . . . shakes at the elbows and knees . . . and . . . bends its impotent black head as . . . [the] song sweeps triumphant" (76) through the mill. If their song briefly unites the workers, unrelieved deprivation ultimately creates schisms within their ranks that ensure the owners' hegemony. And so, though potentially revolutionary, "the pretty song creeps, wounded, back for the engines in the deserted dark to crunch." "The melody of the voices" likewise vanishes "with the vanquished song," and the workers' speech once again becomes "hoarse and rough" (77).

With this world as a backdrop, Sip's and Perley's conversations, while initially exemplifying their respective roles as worker and owner, begin to map alternative kinds of speech between hands and owners. Perley typifies the insensitivity of the mill owners as she sits in her father's library during a storm reveling in her comfort while others suffer because of the weather. Placing "her two hands like sheets of rice-paper over his own" (13), her fiancé, Maverick, ensures that Perley's avowed "weakness for an occupation" (12) will not be fulfilled and that she will remain enshrined in the protected atmosphere in which the mill owners live. The language spoken in the library is as empty as Perley's experience there. Her friend Fly's voice is "like boiling candy" (14) and, as she talks, Perley listens "lazily" to its sound rather than its content. Focusing on the "idle, soft, and sweet" (16) sound of Fly's voice, Perley absents herself from the conversation by drifting off to sleep. She decides to converse with Sip in order to relieve the tedium that results from the seamless affluence that surrounds her in the library. While "watching . . . [the] many muddy people . . . that . . . the sleet did not wash . . . as fast as the mud spattered," Perley finds particularly entertaining "the manful struggles of a girl . . . who . . . struck out with her hands as a boxer would" (17). Sip's voice, like her hands, attests to a struggle against economic and environmental elements about which Perley is ignorant. Noting that "the girl's lips moved angrily, and that she said something in a sharp voice which the wind must have carried the other way" (17), Perley asks Sip to talk to her in order to satisfy her curiosity about the words she missed. Expecting the girl's talk to entertain her, Perley instead feels compelled to reconsider the extent to which her affluence depends upon the condition of the laboring people she watches.

In Phelps's text it is the talk of the working girl, rather than that of the bourgeois woman, that proves most persuasive. Through a series of discussions about the mill, Sip's speech gradually alters both Perley's language and her attitudes toward labor reform. Suddenly resistant to a morning of sitting in the library, Perley ventures out of the mill town, "following the river almost out of hearing of the mill machinery, and quite into the frozen silence of the upper stream" (41). Surrounded by a silence that suggests the potential for different power relations between worker and owner, Perley once again encounters Sip. As they speak to each other the women recognize the dissimilarity of their experiences, but they also struggle to establish a common ground for conversation. Because she is "at a loss how to pursue the art of conversation" with "an ignorant factory-girl" (44), Perley's clumsy, class-conscious comments are met with Sip's "suppressed laugh of 'discontented labor' " (51). But it is only after Perley attempts to "reintroduce conversation" (51) by telling Sip of her first visit to the mill that the women develop a shared interest. Uttered "with an interrogatory accent" like that of a "puzzled scholar," Perley's comments initiate Sip's account of women's experience in the mills. As she speaks, Sip's rhetorical powers become evident. Filled with a desire to refine the theatrical orations of the actresses she has watched, Sip soon forces Perley to realize that "the girl was not far wrong in fancying that she could 'do it over' " (117). Glancing sideways "at her visitor's face," Sip in turn realizes that her theatrical description of factory life has caused the "old, home-like boundary lines ... [to] waver before" (98) her listener.

It is more specifically Sip's firsthand account of the mill's impact on working girls' voices, speech, and sexuality that converts Perley from a socialite into a reformer. Insisting on the irreconcilable differences between middle-class and working women's experiences of language and their bodies, Sip's talk diverges from standard labor rhetoric but nonetheless moves Perley to reformatory action. Telling of "girls . . . who can't even talk beyond a whisper" (81) because of "a peculiar, dry, rasping cough," which Perley learns later "to recognize as the 'cotton-cough' " (82), Sip specifies both the effects of oppressive labor conditions on women's voices and the resulting impossibility of working women's speech ever resembling that of women reformers. As Sip and Perley walk through the town at night, the discordant voices of immigrant factory girls on the streets epitomize the effect of the mill not only on the sound but on the content of women's speech. The "knots of girls . . . singing . . . fragments of murderous Irish threats; of shattered bits of sweet Scotch songs; of half-broken English brogue; of German gutturals . . . [and] only now and then the shrewd, dry Yankee twang" (118) reinforce Sip's account of the radical dissimilarities between bourgeois and working women's voices and speech. The factory girls' abuse strains not only their speech but by extension their sexual propriety. Describing working women's sexuality as another result of oppressive labor conditions, Sip tells of the temptations of a pretty Scotch girl, Nynee, who has been put "to work next to . . . the miserable Irishman, Jim" (123). Because the managers "put him where the work was" and "didn't bother their heads about the girl," "she spends the day with him . . . [and] gets used to him" (123). Although Nynee is "wildish . . . but a good girl," the temptation of the situation, according to Sip, will prove too much for a person otherwise deprived of pleasure, and "she'll go to the devil, sure as death" (123). While Nynee's purity is in jeopardy because of circumstance rather than economic want, another factory girl whom the two women meet on the street has already turned to sexual activity as a release from the tedium of labor. Describing Dib as "a wicked little devil" who "knows more wickedness than you've ever *thought* of" (119), Sip reiterates the vast difference in the sexual experiences of working and middle-class women.

Sip's sharp depiction of the effect of labor on women's voices, speech, and sexuality derives in part from the consequences of unchecked labor practices on her own family, especially her sister, Catty. Catty is a product, and for Sip becomes a symbol, of oppressive labor conditions. Forced to work overtime in the mill while pregnant, her mother, Mrs. Garth, prematurely delivered an infant that was deaf and mute. The mother believed that her child's defect was a result of "the noise . . . of the wheels." According to Sip, "She said [the noise] beat about in her head. She come home . . . and say to herself, 'The baby'll never hear in this world unless she hears the wheels'; and . . . it is true enough that Catty hears the wheels; but never anything besides" (96). Forced to listen "for what she never heard" and to speak "that which no man understood" (278), Catty develops an alternative mode of communication with Sip. "Their silent language" "on work-worn fingers" (85) signals both the extremely negative work conditions of women and the possibility of speech unlinked to the power struggle between laborer and owner. The phrase most often exchanged between the sisters, "for love's sake" (85), becomes a special code for desires that exist outside the capitalist economy of wage labor.

Because of her frustrated speech, Catty's sexuality is irrevocably altered by mill work. Speaking with increasing specificity about her sister's sexual behavior, Sip forces Perley to recognize the profound differences between working-class and middle-class women's experience of sexuality. While their "finger-talk" ensures that Sip "can always understand Catty," it cannot control Catty's impulses for sexual adventure. Deprived of other sensory stimuli, Catty resorts to the excitement of walking the streets by herself all night. Sip attempts to specify Catty's sexual habits by telling Perley that "there's times [Catty] slips away from me . . . there's times she doesn't come till late" (82). Faced with Perley's continued puzzlement, Sip tries again to explain the "things you couldn't understand" by telling of being "turned off on account of Catty" (84). After exclaiming that "I *told* you there's things you couldn't understand," Sip proceeds to specify them by saying that "Catty's queer. . . . She runs away . . . sometimes she drinks, . . . there's sometimes she does – worse" (84). Only after Perley repeats the euphemism "worse" uncertainly does "the young lady's *pure*, puzzled face" drop "suddenly" with recognition (84–5; emphasis added). Forced to hear for the first time a description of female sexuality that conflicts with the "purity" of her own, Perley finally recognizes the distinct consciousness and conditions that define the lives of wage-earning women.

Perley's advocacy of laboring women results from her dawning understanding of the ways in which working women's sexual desires, problematic as they are to the middle-class notion of women's unifying purity, stimulate lives otherwise deprived of sensual experience and pleasure. The dirt that surrounds and defines working women alters their desires, according to Sip. Claiming that "I don't suppose you'd ever guess how much difference the dirt makes" (82), Sip proceeds to highlight its effects on her sister. Pointing to Catty, she exclaims, "That's the difference! To be born in it, breathe it, swallow it, grow on it, live it, die and go back to it . . . – If you want to go to the devil, work in the dirt. Look at her!" (88). Looking at Catty forces Perley to recognize in grim detail the extent to which women's desires are inevitably the product of the work they do. Resisting Sip's request that she come inside rather than seek sensory excitement on the streets, Catty justifies her impulse for public roving "with a shrewd, unpleasant smile" (87). As she stands "scowling . . . a sullen, ill-tempered, ill-controlled, uncontrollable Catty . . . as one could ask to see" (85), Sip's sister signifies the extent to which mill work, on the one hand, deprives its women workers of the full use of their senses and, on the other hand, produces illicit and compensatory desires in them because of that deprivation. Yet Perley's sympathy for Catty is provoked rather than obscured by the physical and sexual "ugliness" that Catty so powerfully displays. Once forced to "look at her . . . very loathsome under lip [and] . . . not pleasant eyes" (88), Perley is rendered momentarily speechless. Her tears become an expression of empathy and advocacy for even the most sexually repulsive working women, and so emend the reactions of prototypical labor reformers when faced with working women's sexual difference.

Though Perley is initially speechless when forced to recognize that working women's desires contradict reformers' interpretative paradigms, her subsequent speech is transformed by her realization. Speech becomes her work, and she learns both to advocate for a labor reform sensitive to working women's differences and to articulate her heightened awareness about her own desires. While Perley initially feels that she has "no words to say how these people seem to me to have been thrust upon my hands" (139), her subsequent conversations with Mr. Garrick, a self-made partner in the mill, and with Maverick register the results of her labor. Because of Garrick's wage-earning background and his resulting inability to "find any dainty words" with which to describe his "passion" (145) "to bring other people . . . out of the mud" (146), Perley is able to perfect, in her talk with him, her own ideas about reform. Sensitive to the clumsy evolution her language undergoes to express her ideas, Perley shares with Garrick her earliest frustrations about the reformatory apathy of the other mill owners. Once she starts to voice her reform agenda publicly, Perley and Maverick's latent incompatibility intensifies, and Perley breaks off their engagement. Refusing Maverick's self-serving conflation of her competing commitments, she tells him to "never mind about the poor little factory girls . . . it is *you* that I do not love" (160). Perley's labor reform work finally enables her to assert her feelings concisely to Maverick and, with a verbal "thrust which even Maverick Hayle could not lightly parry" (160), to insist that he recognize her emotional autonomy.

While Perley's speech reflects her altered perspective, it also serves as an example to Sip of the middle-class language she must master in order to become a successful public speaker. Claiming that she learned how to speak in the mill, Sip insists on the constitutive effect of mill work on her consciousness. Sip's language acquisition contributes to her inability to "feel clean" (201) because it has been tinged with the ever-present "dirt" of the mills. After asserting that "I learned to swear when I learned to talk," Sip expresses a desire to redirect the language that she acquired onto her teachers by calling "curses down on . . . a woman that I used to know for the way she talked to little girls" (202). Yet after listening to Perley speak, Sip realizes that she needs to add bourgeois refinement to her talk if she wants a career as a public speaker. While Perley's words, uttered "with the instinct of a lady" (22), initially prove "remarkable" to Sip, her talent for oratory is subsequently nurtured first passively and then actively during the evenings of "culture" that Perley conducts in her parlor. Sip is initially part of the audience that listens to Perley's playing and recitations, but her long-held desire to "do it over" (117) leads Sip to adopt a performative role. Her readings from Victor Hugo quickly become the most highly acclaimed performances among her diverse listeners. The blend of high culture and populist politics resonates with the workers and middle class alike, and Perley admits that "we have nothing so popular . . . as that girl's reading and recitations." Sip's powerful combination of wage-earning and "cultivated" speech suggests to Perley that "there might be greater than Siddons in Sip . . . but not altogether of the Siddons sort" (233).

It is Sip's rhetorical ability to approximate the codes of middle-class speech while retaining the working woman's experiential perspective on labor that makes Sip's subsequent career as a public speaker successful. Pivotal to her decision to become a public speaker is Catty's death. Left alone in their apartment while Sip shops, Catty, now almost blind, is drawn to the flooding river by its familiar noise. Unable to remain at home, Catty is drowned by the river that drives the mill and so finally becomes a complete victim of uncontrolled labor forces. If, while alive, Catty "spoke that which no man understood" (278), once dead, she becomes "grandly eloquent" (280) not only to Sip but, through Sip's speech, to a larger public. Because "Catty had never talked like other people" (280) and the sisters found other ways to communicate, they cannot "be parted like two speaking people" (279). Sip is thus spared "the *silence* of death" because Catty continues to find ways "to speak to her" (279–80). Believing that Catty talks to her and that "there's things she'd have me say" (291), Sip attends religious meetings. Initially taking the floor as Catty's surrogate voice to communicate the "things [that Catty] had to say" (292), Sip also realizes that "there's been more than I could say" ever since "I saw the people's faces, lifted up and listening . . . when I talked and talked . . . Catty's words" (292). Catty's words of sensual frustration and compensatory desire, once placed in a middle-class religious context, ensure Sip's success as a public speaker. Her blend of "God's words" with "Catty's words" (292) forms a compelling narrative reinforced by the more genteel mannerisms that she has acquired. The hands that Sip initially curled into fists she learns to hold sedately "together at the knuckles" (294) as she speaks. The style proves rhetorically effective, and the middle-class women onlookers are forced to admit that "there was a syntax in Sip's brown . . . and bent hands" (295).

The Politics of Identity and Difference

While Sip's public speech blends multiple experiences, Perley's commentary on it illustrates Phelps's vision of middle-class women's role in the 1870s labor reform movement. As Perley watches Sip speak, she admits to Fly that "I undertook to help her at the first . . . but I was only among them at best; Sip is of them; she understands them and they understand her; so I left her to her work, and I keep to my own" (293). Willing to help Sip, Perley nevertheless realizes the importance of shared experience between reformer and audience. Perley notes the limits of her own empathy when she tells Fly that "we do not understand – we who never need" (301). While Perley, as Phelps's model reformer, has not let the middle-class ideology of purity, with its undercurrent of abhorrence for sexual difference, impede her understanding of working women's psychic and sexual conditions, Sip's public speech highlights the unavoidable limits of Perley's ability to dissociate herself from the gender ideology defining her class in order to reform labor. Sip's public speech, though sanctioned by Perley, finally reiterates the unbridgeable distinctions between the women's classes. The narrator intrudes to insist that the middle-class reader take part in the final consolidation of class distinctions, when she asserts that "in that little court Sip was eloquent . . . on the parlor sofa, in clean cuffs and your slippers, she harangues you" (295).

Sip and Perley's joint effort to expand their public speech in order to revolutionize relations between wage-earning and middle-class women operates as the benchmark of reformatory progress in the text. Yet the final unbridgeable rhetorical distinctions between the two women, rather than subverting the reformatory politics of the text, display its most powerful revisionist goal. As I have shown, Perley's activism, unlike that of other middle-class women reformers, acknowledges rather than erases or vilifies wage-earning women's experience and thereby offers a departure from the labor reform practiced by bourgeois women throughout the 1870s. Yet Phelps finally imagines even this enlightened middle-class reform entirely replaced by the political agitation of working women who identify themselves as a politically significant entity in their own right. With its final chapter devoted to the wage-earning preacher and her audience of workers, Phelps's text offers the earliest vision of women's working-class solidarity that would propel wage-earning women into the center of their own labor reform movement by the 1890s.

6

"Queer Trimmings"

Dressing, Cross-dressing, and Woman's Suffrage in Lillie Devereux Blake's *Fettered for Life*

[Women] find themselves voiceless in the making of the laws . . . having large interests at stake, they find their tongues tied and their hands fettered.

Mark Twain, *Europe and Elsewhere* (1873)

In his sartorial history entitled *The Psychology of Clothes* (1930), J. C. Flügel states that traditionally "clothes reform tends to receive support from the generally rebellious, as a welcome symbolic expression of revolt."[1] Certainly woman suffrage advocates throughout the nineteenth century relied on the rhetoric of dress reformers to reinforce their demands that, as Mark Twain and other equal-rights advocates phrase it, women's tongues be untied and their political voices heard.[2] Arguing that their traditional dress codes amplified the physical differences that supposedly made women "naturally" unsuitable for political responsibility, suffrage proponents suggested that women adopt male attire in order to free themselves from their social and political "fetters." Drawing on the numerous autobiographical accounts of women who cross-dressed in order to serve as soldiers in the Civil War and the increasingly common accounts in newspapers after 1850 of "the deaths of men who turned out to be women,"[3] equal-rights proponents claimed that female transvestitism, because it disguised the physical differences that made women subservient to unscrupulous men, ensured not only women's political equality but their sexual purity as well.

However, by "discovering" the female sexual invert,[4] late-

nineteenth- and early-twentieth-century sexologists effectively neutralized the increasing political power of the woman's suffrage
movement. Unlike Victorian reformers who contended that the
"tendency . . . to adopt male attire"[5] denoted women's purity, sexologists claimed instead that women's transvestitism indicated their
sexual inversion or impurity. They proceeded to attack "the modern
movement of emancipation" by arguing that, if not "directly the
cause of sexual inversion," women's suffrage at the very least "develop[ed] the germs of it" (Ellis, 1:100). Claiming that women who
have "been taught independence of men" tend "to carry this independence still further and . . . find love where they find work"
(1:100), Havelock Ellis and other sexologists, by the early twentieth
century, effectively transformed the cross-dressing suffragette, according to cultural historians, into "a sexual anomaly and a political
pariah."[6]

Using as a starting point sexologists' "discovery," at the turn into
the twentieth century, of the sexually impure and therefore politically ineffective female invert, scholars of nineteenth-century American culture have concluded that the political power wielded by
Victorian women depended upon the passionlessness of their relations not only with men but, by extension, with women.[7] Yet, like
the sexological "discovery" on which they depend, these cultural
historical studies tend to ignore the nineteenth-century women political activists who resisted dominant Victorian models of femininity. In short, they overlook the nineteenth-century cross-dressing
woman who gains political as well as sexual freedom by passing as a
man.[8] Inheriting from sexologists a powerful conceptual framework
for interpreting the history of women's desire, scholars of
nineteenth-century American culture thus have inadvertently
tended to produce accounts of women's relations and political activism that reflect prevailing models rather than the full range of
social influences.[9]

Yet because sexologists' purported discovery of the female invert,
as I will show, draws heavily on Victorian depictions of women cross-
dressers, reassessing those accounts, and more particularly Lillie
Devereux Blake's fictional portrayal of the woman transvestite as an

equal-rights advocate, expands our understanding not only of the nineteenth-century woman's suffrage movement's political power but of the origins of early-twentieth-century accounts of women's political power. In this chapter, as in the preceding three, I show how a woman writer foregrounds the female voice and women's public speech in her own public narrative in order to maximize its political impact. Like Elizabeth Stuart Phelps, Lillie Devereux Blake advocates for political change by creating a woman whose public speech is motivated by, and effectively represents, the distorted voices of women made vulnerable, in this case, by the femininity of their clothing. However, I show in addition that Blake's suffrage narrative and the cultural texts it engages create an important historical context in which to place subsequent sexological accounts of female subjectivity that, by ignoring their indebtedness to nineteenth-century social influences, are able to neutralize suffrage activists' political sway.[10] Written before sexologists created the discourse of inversion that would strip the transvestite of political power, *Fettered for Life* (1874) shows how a cross-dressing suffragette's homoerotic ties empower, rather than impede, her political advocacy.[11] In so doing, Blake's text complicates existing narratives of both nineteenth- and early-twentieth-century woman's suffrage activism that tend to identify women's same-sex desire and its impact on the woman's suffrage movement as distinctly twentieth-century phenomena. And so, once placed in the context of contemporary accounts of women's dressing and cross-dressing, *Fettered for Life* expands existing models of suffrage proponents' political rhetoric in both nineteenth- and twentieth-century America.

"Ever at Masquerade"

Throughout the nineteenth century, dress reformers contended that women's clothing obscured, rather than enhanced, the passionlessness from which bourgeois women derived much of their social and political power. In *The Excellency of the Female Character Vindicated* (1807) Thomas Branagan, for example, outlines the deleterious effects of female fashion on nineteenth-century femininity. According to Branagan, even "ladies high in estimation" become "slaves" to the "most obscene and indecent" fashions, and so end up strutting "through the streets, with the disgraceful and obscene appearances peculiar to lewd women."[12] Until "laws [are] enacted to keep female fashions within the bounds of common decency; and to fix the distinction between lewd and virtuous women" (18), Branagan contends that all women will be susceptible to the attention of America's sexually excited men. Indeed, it is the public perambulations of "virtuous and . . . reputable ladies," in dress "more indecent than the vilest prostitutes," that "not only . . . entice[s], but almost . . . force[s] the male of ardent passions to acts of violence, as well as to the arts of seduction" (18). And so, threatened by the sexually aggressive behavior of overstimulated men, middle-class women are forced to curtail their public appearances and political activity.

To recover the physical freedom and political equality denied them by their traditional dress, suffrage advocates argue that women should consider donning bloomers and even complete male disguises.[13] Sarah Grimke was the first to assert that women's dress plays a pivotal role in sustaining women's political inequity when, in *Letters on the Equality of the Sexes* (1838), she admits: "I do believe one of the chief obstacles in the way of woman's elevation to the same platform of human rights . . . with her brother . . . is her love of dress. . . . [S]o long as we submit to be dressed like dolls, we never can rise to the station of duty . . . from which [men] desire to exclude us."[14] In his 1855 correspondence with Elizabeth Cady Stanton, Gerrit Smith likewise contends that equality between the sexes will never be achieved unless every "woman attire[s] her person fitly for the whole battle of life," which "she is as much bound to fight as man is."[15] Commenting on the "radical revolution in female costume . . . made in America"[16] that Smith's daughter initiated with her bloomers, Mrs. Oliphant, in her 1879 manual, *Dress*, highlights not the sexual but the physical restrictions created by women's clothes. Asserting that "the bondage of [women's] dress at times reaches . . . the extravagance of preventing movement altogether, so that a lady . . . can hardly walk [and] can only with difficulty get up stairs" (70), Mrs. Oliphant concludes that the "whole female race," because it is "more or less tied into narrow bags," becomes a "painful spectacle" in need of sartorial liberation (43). In her autobiography, Elizabeth Cady Stanton admits that it was the "difficulty" of climbing upstairs "with flowing robes," compared with "the ease and grace" with which her bloomer-clad cousin ascends the stairs, holding "a lamp in one hand and a baby in the other," that convinced her of the need for dress reform.[17] The two years that Stanton subsequently spent in bloomers satisfied her that mannish clothing offered "incredible freedom" (201) to its wearers. A "woman is terribly cramped and crippled in her present style of dress," she concluded, and therefore "should dress just like a man ... [to] enjoy entire freedom" (Kraditor, 129). Invoking the ability of "the distinguished French woman, George Sand," "to see life" and to "[speak] in political meetings" (129), Stanton wonders whether transvestitism might not offer American women greater physical and sexual freedom as well. She speculates that, "in male attire, we could travel by land or sea, [and] go through all the streets and lanes of our cities and towns by night and day ... without fear of insult, or the least sacrifice of decency or virtue" (129). Concluding that "if nature has not made the sex so clearly defined as to be seen through any disguise, why should we make the difference so striking?" (130), Stanton implies that because transvestitism can succeed it should succeed.

Elizabeth Cady Stanton's interest in the sexual and physical freedom that transvestitism offers women reflected a more general Victorian interest in women whose successful male disguise enabled them to engage fully in public and political life. Menie Muriel Dowie's nostalgic reflections on the cross-dressing woman in *Women Adventurers* (1893), for example, suggest the enduring importance of the transvestite for the nation's fantasies about the illicit power enjoyed by a few of its women. Bemoaning the way that "women who step out of the ranks to-day and go forth adventuring, do it in all the cold seriousness of skirts,"[18] Dowie argues that the woman "adventurer" of the mid-nineteenth century offers an appealing alternative for political activism. Confessing that "the fine female blusterer['s]" greater political effectiveness results from her "being

ever at masquerade," Dowie admits to preferring "the picturesque-
ness" of the woman adventurer's appearance and "the dashing poetry of her swagger" (xx). "Passing for a man most of the time," the
woman transvestite exhibits her superior shrewdness by "imitating"
his "bearing" so successfully that she is never " 'discovered' " (xx).
And so, because she is able to pass for a man, the woman adventurer
takes part in all aspects of male culture and enjoys the social and
political privileges about which other women continue to fantasize.

While her physical appearance is convincing, it is the public
speech of the cross-dressing woman that completes her disguise and
ensures that she will intercede effectively in politics. In her *Woman
in Battle* (1876), Loreta Velazquez argues that many women's public
speech can pass as male because "so many men have weak and
feminine voices."[19] Thus, even a woman with "a very high-pitched
voice need have very little fear" of discovery, "provided the clothing
is . . . put on right, and the disguise in other respects is well-
arranged" (5). Nevertheless, the ease with which the voices of
women transvestites pass as male indicates exceptional vocal capabil-
ity. Equipped with only her "exquisite though uncultivated voice,
the soft, winning notes of which were as free and unrestrained as
one of her prairie birds,"[20] Pauline Cushman, for example, is able
to begin a "battle with [the] great world" (35) that leads her quickly
into the Civil War. Heeding her "little yet all powerful inner voice"
(67), Cushman cross-dresses in order to join the Union army and
then proceeds to talk people into relating vital information. In his
1866 biography of Deborah Sampson, *The Female Review,* John Vinton likewise claims that Sampson began as a child to make "herself
mistress of pronunciation and sentences" by "listen[ing] to everyone
. . . [who] read[s] and speak[s] with propriety."[21] Eventually her
"deliberate" speech and "firm articulation" make her seem a "masculine and serene," rather than an "effeminate" (134), man. In
Unsexed: Or, The Female Soldier (1864), Emma E. Edmonds describes
the various "tone[s] of voice"[22] that she assumes as she changes
male disguises in order to glean information from the enemy. In the
process, she becomes quick to detect other women's vocal and
sartorial masquerades as well. Hearing "in the tone and voice" of a

disguised woman "something" that makes Edmonds "look more closely at the face of the speaker" (271), she discovers another cross-dressed woman spy and so wins accolades on the battlefield.

Once these women are able to engage successfully in public life, they, according to the numerous popular accounts written by and about women cross-dressers, use their public sway to protect the sexual purity[23] of women made vulnerable by their feminine clothing. For example, John Vinton claims that Deborah Sampson joined the Revolutionary army for just this reason. Upon learning "that many of her own sex were either ravished, or deluded to sacrifice their chastity," Sampson experiences "sensations, to which she had hitherto been unaccustomed" (78). Because her aim is to preserve the passionlessness of her American sisters, Sampson's adoption of male clothes reinforces, rather than calls into question, her femininity. According to Vinton, "Prudence . . . appeared in her plain, but neat attire . . . delicacy trimmed her dislocated hair; and virtue brought her a wreathe" as she "dressed herself in a handsome suit of man's apparel" (115). Because she is able to "mingl[e] constantly with men, day and night, in all their exercises, through so many months," while maintaining "her virtue unsullied" (xxx), Sampson protects other women from sexual abuse throughout the war. Even once her "true" sex is discovered, she admits in her journal to "prefer[ring] my regimentals, because in them I should be more safe from insult" (221) and so, by continuing to cross-dress, she protects her own purity as well.

However, while women cross-dressers use male disguises to uphold and protect women's sexual purity, they consistently acknowledge that their transvestitism satisfies unspecific but irresistible desires. Once she hears of the endangered purity of American women, Deborah Sampson is "filled . . . with a kind of enthusiasm" (Vinton, 78) to adopt a male disguise, but she later admits, according to Vinton, that enlisting "as a soldier" is the only "method for gratifying the roving propensities which had now acquired full possession of her mind" (117). Asserting that "none . . . could take cognisance of the effusions of passion" that Sampson experienced "on assuming her new garb" (126), Vinton concludes that while "there is no denying that she felt the impulse of patriotism, . . . this seems not to have been the principal motive" (117) behind her decision to cross-dress. In *The Woman in Battle* Loreta Velazquez claims that "the principal motive" behind her own "overmastering desire . . . to assume the dress of the other sex" is "enjoyment" (20). Yet immediately adding "if I can designate my peculiar emotions by such a word" (20), Velazquez registers the inability of existing linguistic codes to describe her feelings. She nonetheless specifies their intensity, writing, "Ridicule, as well as danger, was what I resolved to brave when putting on male attire, and I really dreaded it less than I did my own heart burnings" (16) in the event of remaining in women's clothes.

The compelling but unspecifiable desires that led women to cross-dress often resulted in the intimate female relations that sexologists would later identify as sexually inverted. Yet, because nineteenth-century audiences were not influenced by sexological discourses, they recognized, but defined as "platonic," physical intimacy between women, and so the homoerotic bonds of women cross-dressers enhanced rather than disabled their public activity. "Everywhere received as a blithe, handsome, and agreeable young gentleman" (Vinton, 129), Sampson, for example, inspires a "giddy passion" (191) in a young woman. Thinking that she is in love with a man, Miss P___ agrees to consummate their relationship, and they finally become "mutually and tenderly attached" by "reciprocat[ing] their love amidst the dews of dawn" (191). According to Vinton, women readers likewise are susceptible to Sampson's "dazzling enchantments" and so are "ready to yield the pride and ornament of [their] sex" (243) to her. Although Miss P___ may be fooled by Sampson's male attire into a same-sex liaison, Sampson's homoerotic desires prove to be more overt. While insisting that "sickness had abated [Sampson's] acuteness for . . . love," Vinton nonetheless admits that Sampson "doubtless embraced the celestial maid and could not but participate in the genial warmth of [the] passion" (198). Later, when her "irresistible attraction" draws her "again to the presence of the amiable Miss P___" (213), rather than "confess-[ing] to her who and what I was," Sampson instead resumes their relations, and so the "two lovers [part], more . . . constant than" ever (214). The homoerotic "passion" that sexologists would clearly identify as sexually inverted by the early twentieth century is described as "laudable" (215) by Sampson's biographer. Indeed, any woman who engages in sexual relations with Sampson, whether in "fact" or in fantasy, "preserves inviolate . . . [her] virginity" (243). Thus, because the nineteenth-century woman's "correspondence with her sister sex" is characterized by a "purity" that makes "animal love, on her part out of the question" (225), the woman crossdresser has the authority to intervene in the political and public life from which she would be marginalized by the twentieth-century medical discourse of sexual inversion.

Sexologists completed their marginalization of the woman transvestite by transforming her remarkable ability to imitate men's speech into a definitive sign of her sexual inversion as well. According to Havelock Ellis, sexually inverted women exhibit "a very pronounced tendency . . . to adopt male attire" (1:95), as well as to imitate male modes of speech. Ellis concurs with Richard Von Krafft-Ebing's claim in *Psychopathia Sexualis* (1893) that the woman invert's "rough deep voice . . . betray[s] rather the man than the woman."[24] Having asserted that "the direct speech, the inflexions of the voice" suggest women who "ought to have been men" (1:96), Ellis goes on to argue that the difference in the "tone of the voice" is due to "anatomical modification" and then to cite the work of a scientist who "examined the larynx in twenty-three inverted women, and found in several a very decidedly masculine type of larynx" (97). Thus, by claiming that the woman cross-dresser's voice as well as clothing indicates her sexual inversion, sexologists helped to silence the political voices of many of the most adventurous female reformers of the nineteenth century.

However, because Lillie Devereux Blake wrote *Fettered for Life* (1874) before sexological discourses of inversion politically marginalized the cross-dressing suffragette, she was able to advocate for equal rights, first, by insisting that it is the femininity, rather than the masculinity, of women's voices and dress that is responsible for their political powerlessness and, second, by creating a cross-dressing suffragette who uses the public speech to which she is subsequently entitled as a man to defend women whose public silence is produced and represented by their distorted voices. Blake punctuated her career as a public champion of women's labor reform and suffrage by writing,[25] according to some scholars, "the most comprehensive women's rights novel of the nineteenth century."[26] By depicting a woman who uses her powerful public speech to represent silenced women and defend their right to "gain a voice," Blake convinces her readers of the need for suffrage. Yet the compelling vision of sexual, vocal, and political equity with which the novel closes depends on the female transvestite, Frank Heywood, and more particularly on the alliance she forges with Laura Stanley.[27] In this relationship the closeness that, according to scholars, defines nineteenth-century female relations combines with the same-sex desires that sexologists claim originated in the twentieth century in order to equip women to demand the equality they deserve. And so, by structuring her text's political advocacy around the intimate, erotic relationship in which her cross-dressing heroine engages, Blake not only complicates existing models of women's relations and political influence in Victorian America but, in so doing, provides a historical context in which to place and reconsider the sexological accounts of women suffragettes that effectively neutralized their political impact by the early twentieth century.

"Stopping Their Talk"

Fettered for Life tracks the parallel and overlapping careers of a reporter, Frank Heywood, and an artist, Laura Stanley.[28] Though drawn to New York by professional opportunities, once there both women encounter extreme sexism that finally threatens their professional and personal lives. Frank responds to the paucity of opportunities available to women by transforming herself into a man and pursuing a successful career as a newspaper reporter. Her job brings her into contact with many women abused by a public culture that denies them legal and social equality, but it is her developing relationship with Laura that structures both Blake's text and its suffrage politics. The intimacy of their friendship increases as Frank teaches Laura how to use her voice to demand equality not only in the professional arena but in the personal negotiations she conducts with her suitor. Because of her empowered speech, Laura achieves the unmitigated respect of her professional colleagues and marriage partner and thus becomes a prime exemplar of the female equality that the vote would publicly acknowledge and protect.

However, Blake begins advocating for women's voting rights in *Fettered for Life* by exploiting the terms in which nineteenth-century woman's suffrage was couched – equating women's desire to gain the vote with their desire to gain the use of their voices and presenting women's political silencing as indicative of a more general refusal to hear women's speech. In the act of voting, men are characterized by Blake as exerting a political agency that is signified and embellished by their "discordant songs, shouted words, and coarse laughter" (154). While "profess[ing] to honor [women's] goodness and purity," the government "refuses [women] all voice" (68), because, as the suffrage activist and prominent doctor Mrs. D'Arcy claims, the otherwise "sensible people" that it represents "seem to think that if we can vote, we shall all grow loud-voiced . . . coarse and masculine" (258). Convinced that denying political voice to women ensures that their outlook and elocution will remain "gentler, purer, and more religious than [men's]" (258), policy makers fail to acknowledge the more pervasive vocal aberrations that result from the suppression of women's political articulations. Thinking "that the agitation of woman suffrage is only the work of a few discontented souls," these men fail to "understand that the demand for political equality is but one of the public utterances of a great dumb cry, that goes up from millions" of women (54).

Indeed, it is these men's tyrannical and sadistic control over women's voices and speech that emerges as the novel's primary justification for giving women the vote. Claiming that "min don't mind what wimmin folks say [because] they don't go to 'lection" (31), the washerwoman Biddy succinctly states the personal impotence produced by women's political voicelessness. Though initially a respectful son to Biddy, once Pat is old enough to vote he learns that he can enforce in the home the silencing of the female voice that he enacts in the voting booth. Thus, Biddy complains that Pat refuses to acknowledge the importance of her words by saying, "Don't ye be a talkin', mither . . . Yer'e only a woman" (30). Marital relations, however, most profoundly replicate the power inequities created by women's lack of a political voice. Mr. Bludgett, for example, enforces his supremacy over his wife by demanding her silence. The "very plaintive . . . trembling voice" (17) in which Mrs. Bludgett capitulates to her husband's oppressive demand reinforces her admission that she does "not have the same right" (18) to voice her opinions as Mr. Bludgett because, as "a man," he is entitled to "use hard words" (19). Bludgett enforces his "words," consisting of "an oath . . . ending with a vile word" (61), by physically abusing his wife. Enraged by his wife's ability to provoke remorse for a murder that he committed and she witnessed, he becomes "absolutely savage" and beats her in an attempt to stop her "snivelling" and "whining" (374). Determined to silence her voice as it pleads for mercy, he stamps "his heavy boot-heel on [her] helpless mouth" (375) and commits a second murder in his attempt to quiet his guilt over the first.

Reassured by women's political voicelessness, Judge Swinton, the most politically powerful and violently misogynistic man in Blake's novel, asserts his corrupt authority by disfiguring the mouth of a woman named Rhoda and then attempting to silence her account of that event. Though she is generally attractive, Rhoda's mouth is left "drawn and drooping, while the loss of two front teeth disfigur[e] a set otherwise white and regular" (56). Rhoda's experience shapes the words she uses. She becomes well known for having "a sharp tongue and a sort of ready wit, that [are] at once fascinating and repellant [sic]" (120). Her verbal canniness equips her to defend herself against the subsequent demands of her abuser. With a "sneering emphasis" to her "fierce words" (124), Rhoda keeps Swinton's account of their affair from becoming the prevailing account. Rejecting his attempt to bribe her into "holding her tongue," Rhoda provides indisputable evidence of the gravity of his crime when, "pointing quickly to her mutilated mouth," she demands, " 'Do you think I have forgotten the coward blow that has disfigured me for life?'" (125). While Rhoda is able to prevent Swinton from suppressing her story, the narrator insists that women's more general "voicelessness" is responsible for the sexual victimage to which Rhoda's mouth and her words bear witness. We must "look ... at poor Rhoda," the narrator asserts, mindful that, "if she were a voter, with influence over voters, she would be treated very differently by men" (257). Without the means to seek redress for her sexual and physical abuse, Rhoda is forced to trade in the male sexuality that appalls and threatens her by working in a saloon, where she must wear dresses "cut low" (117) for the pleasure of male customers who remain "none the worse for saying and doing what stamped her ... with infamy" (121).

In Blake's account, it is women's clothing that signals their lack of a personal as well as political voice. Forced to come to work dressed "low" because her bare shoulders "are worth a dollar a night to" the owner, one of Rhoda's friends tries to "wear just a little scarf round [her] throat" (58) because it is sore. Told that she "can't come covered up like an old woman" (58), the woman exposes her attractive neck until she is seized "with a fit of coughing" and dies from a broken blood vessel. Mrs. Bludgett's clothing likewise makes explicit the abuse that she suffers at the hands of her husband. The "rent" visible in her "dingy black alpaca" (165) is metonymic for the violence done to her flesh by Mr. Bludgett. While her friend's hat is merely last year's style and missing a bow, Mrs. Bludgett's hat rises "very high over her forehead in some absurd past fashion, making her pale face look paler in contrast with the yellow and red roses which filled the space above her scanty hair" (166). Though the relative oppressiveness of women's domestic conditions is gauged by the clothing they wear, Mrs. Bludgett's deteriorating attire signals her impending dissolution. Usually "shabby and dirty" (14), Mrs. Bludgett's costume, on her final house call, is particularly slothful: "Shabbily dressed, ... her wonderful bonnet was on one side; her shawl was dragged up over one shoulder; [and] her dress ... showed traces of street mud" (218). The displaced bonnet and shawl anticipate the bodily dislocations she is about to suffer, while the splashes of mud on her skirt become metonymic for the "spurting . . . blood [that] drop[s] over her pallid face" (375) when her mouth is finally destroyed by her husband's effort to stop her talk.

Women's dress, in addition to reiterating their private voicelessness, forces them, from girlhood, to accept their public silencing. When Mrs. D'Arcy visits a girls' school and discovers an abundance of "pretty delicate creatures" with "transparent complexions [that] indicate a total lack of vitality" (74), she attributes their physical lassitude to the dress they are compelled to wear. Cloaked in "dainty white frocks" that are "the extreme of the latest fashion," their "slender figures" already "show the impress of the corset that [will] mould [their] pliant forms into stylish smallness of waist" (74). Angered by the physical distortions required by stylish women's clothing, Mrs. D'Arcy wants "to strip off the oppressive finery, and the stifling steel-clasped garments" and to replace them with "plain, serviceable frocks" (74) that will allow the girls the freedom of motion that feminine health requires. Likening America's education of women to the Chinese regimen for disciplining them, Mrs. D'Arcy argues that "a fashionable training so hampers a woman's body and mind, that one can no more expect freedom of action [in American women] . . . than one can expect the Chinese ladies with their distorted feet to walk" unhindered (161).[29]

Flora Livingston's career exemplifies how such sartorial constraint contributes to women's inevitable complicity in their own silencing. Flora reveals the extent to which her traditionally aristocratic upbringing has influenced her attitudes regarding femininity and dress, when she admits that she expected Mrs. D'Arcy to "be old-maidish, and wear spectacles and a very short dress" (70) because of her career and suffrage work. Swayed by "conventional caricatures of strong-minded women" (70), Flora is as incapable of altering her preconceptions regarding nontraditional women as she is of changing her own mode of dress. "Attired in the most tasteful of walking suits" (70), Flora appears to be a model of femininity to Ferdinand Le Roy, the most eligible bachelor in New York. Though Flora does not want to marry Le Roy, her father insists that she act as "a true woman" (101). In an effort to elicit Flora's cooperation in his plans for her marriage, Mr. Livingston gives her money "to buy a new dress" for a ball and thereby ensures that "a match will ... result" (103). In her toilette of silk and lace, Flora presents a picture of "dainty loveliness" (126) that Le Roy finds irresistible. Le Roy's marriage proposal and his refusal to hear her response to it initiates the oppressive silencing that Flora will suffer in their marriage. While Flora remains "passive" as Le Roy forces a kiss of acquiescence from her, she experiences "a passionate revolt ... wholly impossible to put ... into words" (128). Though she is incapable of articulating her feelings of sexual revulsion, Ferdinand's kiss nonetheless lies "in her memory ... as a mark of servitude" (147). The mouth with which she kisses Ferdinand becomes the gauge of the resulting sexual revulsion that Flora cannot vocalize. Her "finely formed" mouth, while initially evidencing "great possibilities of passion" (39), becomes distorted. The coercion that Le Roy uses in their first sexual encounter proves characteristic and produces "around [Flora's] mouth ... a shade of disgust" (262). She thus utters her marriage vows with "a shade of blueness around [her] mouth" and with "lips parted as if in some mute entreaty" (245).

Invested in ignoring Flora's feelings and her attempts to "put [them] into words" (128), her family and fiancé strategically assume that Flora's well-being is produced by her clothes. Asking "Are you pale or is it your dress?" (230), Le Roy reads the pallor produced by Flora's disgust for him as the effect of her clothing. By suggesting that she "wear pink, like Maud" (230), Le Roy reminds Flora of the contingency of her value to him and the importance of maintaining that value by dressing to advantage. Able to signify her resistance only by "moaning piteously" and crying with "utter anguish" (241), Flora nonetheless acquiesces to her husband's sartorial demands. "Dressed in a costume of green silk in several shades; a French dress, wonderful in elaborate beauty of design," Flora appears "to the casual observer" to be "the fortunate wife of a wealthy man" (284). In an attempt to overcome the despair produced by the gap between her public appearance and private condition, Flora turns to writing. Yet once again her speech is stymied by Ferdinand, who, in the act of tearing up her poetry, elicits from Flora "a cry as if he had been tearing her own flesh" (334). On her deathbed Flora cites her unhappy marriage as the cause of her impending death, but must still fight her mother's attempt to stifle her speech. Overriding Mrs. Livingston's demand that she not speak "such wild words [because] the doctor has forbidden your talking much," Flora asserts that "they are not wild words, and it will not hurt me to talk now" (351). Yet the effort to voice her domestic unhappiness and sexual disgust for Ferdinand, while finally successful, costs her her life.

"The Caricature That Lurks in Clothes"

By shedding women's clothing and its vocal and sexual constraints, Frank Heywood is able to use his voice to defend women publicly against male oppression.[30] Successfully passing as a man to both fictional and reading audiences, Frank moves through all parts of New York collecting stories for the *Trumpeter*. Acting in the capacity of reporter to and representative of the public, Frank uses the public voice to which his transvestitism gives him access in order to protect the women he encounters on the streets and to curb the actions of men who view those women, because of their personal and political voicelessness, as sexual prey. Mrs. D'Arcy asserts that the "two great professions" open to women are "medicine and journalism" (64). But since one is held by a matron and the other by a cross-dresser, neither seems open to women who traditionally have the greatest sexual appeal to men. When Frank finally reveals her sexual identity at the end of the novel, she justifies her decision to cross-dress by claiming that, because she is "a very good-looking girl," she encountered, when she first arrived in New York wearing women's clothing, persistent persecution from men. Realizing that her "beauty" is hindering her job search, Frank buys "a suit of boy's clothes" (366) and experiences the physical, emotional, and economic freedom conferred by men's garments. Suddenly able to "move untrammeled" in public, Frank visits "places and scenes" that she admits she "could not have visited in the garb of my sex" (366–7). Her greater mobility enables her to report and so police acts of sexism that occur outside the public's surveillance. The compatibility between Frank's journalistic and feminist projects, combined with an account she reads "of [a] physician ... who died and was discovered to be a woman" (366), results in Frank's determination to make her masquerade permanent. Initially appearing in the text as "a good-looking young man, apparently about twenty-five, with ... [a] chestnut moustache, shading a mouth that, but for this, would have been effeminate" (10), Frank first uses his authority as vocalizer of news stories to protect the ill-clad saloon girls detained and freezing in the local jail. Seeing that they "had only light shawls and cloaks," Frank tells the women's jailer, in a voice that "was grand to hear," that if they aren't "made warm and comfortable, he'll put an item in the paper about it" (58).

While Frank defends women with a public speech empowered by both his vocal and sartorial masquerade, his extended interactions with Laura Stanley allow him to enjoy fully the physical adventure and sexual invulnerability that characterize the nineteenth-century cross-dresser's experience, according to the accounts of dress reformers and transvestites. Because of her father's domestic tyranny, Laura decides to leave her affluent home and support herself in the city. Invested in female silence as a sign of his hegemony, Mr. Stanley makes his "presence [felt as] an oppression; chilling [his daughters'] mirth, stopping their talk" (318). Mr. Stanley exerts his authority most powerfully at the dinner table, where he silences the "suppressed conversation" that begins among the women by demanding his tea. While Mr. Stanley's words ensure that "scarcely a word was spoken" (316) for the rest of the meal, his mere approach causes "the ripple of girlish laughter [to] die away, and frigid silence [to] reign" (318). Mr. Stanley's despotism is characterized not only by "hard words" (33) but by the deteriorating clothing that his wife and daughters wear. Though "with all [his] broad acres ... her father [is] amply able to give the girls ... suitable clothing" (313), Mr. Stanley makes his daughters wear "faded calicoes" and "plainly dressed ... holland suits" (311–13). Mrs. Stanley's ill-conceived ensemble, composed of "a dark calico dress, a long black silk sacque of some past fashion, a plain bonnet and a green veil, which she was holding on with her mouth" (311), indicate both her economic deprivation and servitude to her husband. Forced to work constantly because Mr. Stanley refuses to spend money on domestic help, Mrs. Stanley never has time to arrange her garments, which remain continually askew. Laura's attempts to "put to rights" her mother's crooked collar and to fasten the veil that her mother holds in place with her teeth, while immediately helpful, fail to resolve the larger inequity of which the Stanley women's clothing is a symptom.

Though Laura flees to the city to escape her father's tyranny, her dress and voice make her immediately subject to the same oppressive male authority that she is attempting to elude. Arriving after nightfall without a place to stay, Laura is accosted by men from whom she requests help and finally finds refuge at the local police station. Rounded up with the prisoners, Laura finds herself before Judge Swinton, who, because of the quality of her clothing and speech, marks her out as his next sexual victim. Though grouped with "miserable prisoners [who] shiver in their wretched garments," Laura, "neatly, but very plainly dressed," stands out from the other women, who are "gaudily habited" (7). While her dress is "simple," "there [is] an indescribable something in the arrangement of the luxuriant brown hair, in the neat white ruffle at the throat, in the look of the pretty traveling satchel which she carried, that indicated refinement" (8). When asked to account for her homelessness, Laura's "accent, her modes of expression, the tones of her voice" likewise identify her as "an educated lady" (9) and so undermine her claim that she is a domestic laborer. The sartorial and linguistic traces of refinement both pique Swinton's sexual interest and suggest to him that he can gratify it. Identifying Laura as an abandoned and therefore defenseless woman, Swinton plots to abduct her. After Frank knocks him down and escapes with Laura, the judge attempts to win Laura through coercion rather than compulsion. Judge Swinton both explains and apologizes for his criminal behavior by telling Laura that "your dress was so plain that I was deceived as to your real rank" (88). Frank saves Laura from a second abduction by waylaying and entering the carriage in which she is confined. Opening the carriage door in the full expectation of seeing "a pale and swooning girl," the judge is instead face to face with "Frank Heywood's alert figure" (190). Announcing himself as "a reporter for the New York *Trumpeter*," Frank threatens to "make an item of this for the paper if you like, Judge" (190). Thus, brashly replacing the silence of the drugged woman with the voice of the *Trumpeter*, Frank enjoys the physical and sexual freedom of his disguise while defending Laura's sexual purity.

During the friendship that subsequently flourishes, Frank protects Laura not only by wielding his public voice but by teaching her how to control her own voice in order to speak with authority. Sensitive to the fact that it is his "clear young voice" (22) that enables Frank to "resent" the judge's rude and insolent speech on her behalf, Laura becomes "fascinated strangely" both with the range of Frank's conversation and with "the tones of his low musical voice" (48). "Confiding in him in a way that surprised her" (48), Laura admits to her own impulses to join in "the cry [of rage] that has gone up from so many women" (64). Listening to Frank speak makes Laura realize that she is often "less cautious in her utterances than [is] always wise" (18). With increasing self-consciousness she admits, "I am so apt, in arguments . . . to lose my temper, and say sharp things, instead of really answering objections" (254). Because they "think [Laura] would know what to say" (248), her female students ask her to present to the schoolmaster their petition to give their own public address on the last day of school. Though she persuasively presents the facts to get his endorsement of the plan, the schoolmaster's sexism enrages Laura, whose "quick temper" leads her to "imprudent speech" (251) and thus causes the students' plan to be vetoed. Remorseful as she later describes the situation, Laura admits that she "was dreadfully imprudent [and] . . . ought not to have spoken" (254) so rashly. Gradually attuning herself to her rhetorical shortcomings, Laura becomes increasingly able to adjust the manner in which she speaks to her audience. After a heated discussion about suffrage, for example, Laura makes sure that she has not alienated her listener, asking if "you will think me terribly fierce, Mr. Bradford, to be talking so strongly on this subject" (67).

Laura's increased ability to speak effectively safeguards her from the kind of oppressive marriage to which her more vocally timid friend, Flora, is condemned. While Guy Bradford is "full of unspoken . . . passion" (245) for Laura and "long[s] to testify his sympathy in words" (52), his actual speech does not further his suit. Guy tries to assert his proprietorship over Laura by invoking the repressive dress codes against which women like Frank and Mrs. D'Arcy so actively struggle. Guy admits to Laura in a "somewhat imperious" tone (293) that he "only wish[es] you could wear a veil; that is, provided you took it off for me" (206). While Guy, "manlike . . . [thinks] of nothing . . . but the passion that absorb[s] him" (282), Laura remains as disturbed by what Guy does not say as by what he does say. Simultaneously annoyed by both the content and vagueness of Guy's words and his expectation that they adequately communicate his feelings, Laura silences him by asserting that she "cannot make all sorts of admissions in reply to a few vague words" (283). When Guy finally speaks, his preemptive demand that Laura tell him where she spent her first night in New York causes her to silence and dismiss him. Laura's refusal to enter a relationship characterized by linguistic and sexual inequity forces Guy to consider his attitudes and to realize that he needs "to pick [his] words" (292) carefully if he wants a life with Laura. Admitting that he has no "right to ask" Laura for "a strict account of every act of her life" and that "in the sight of God, men and woman are equal" (378), Guy again attempts "to win from her own lips an answer to his question" (379). But this time he asks her to marry him without demanding an account of her sexual past and with a commitment to a relationship based on mutual trust in which both partners are "equals in all things" (379).

Laura's transformation of dress, as well as the vocal equity she achieves, signals the parity of her relationship with Guy. Though Flora attempts to alter Laura's "dreadful" hat when they first meet in New York, Laura asserts that her friend "can't make me stylish on any terms" (40). Laura's poverty, as much as her rural background, keep her from dressing fashionably. Because she refuses to rely on others for clothing money, the condition of her garments indicates her financial status. After working hard to support herself, Laura is finally able to "purchase for the first time in nearly a year, a new dress . . . tastefully made, the dark blue trimmings with which it was ornamented . . . giving the costume a tint and character" (279). Taking "unusual pains with her dress" (279), Laura, at the art opening honoring her work, appears not only as an attractive but as a financially independent young artist. She thus "acquire[s] that indescribable air of style which had once been wanting in her appearance" (279) as much through her increasingly sophisticated aesthetic sensibilities as through her increasingly successful career. Armed with "a trunk containing a renovated wardrobe . . . the cost of which she had earned every penny" (362), Laura is able to look her best without sacrificing her economic autonomy. Indeed, her stylish dressing signals the achievement rather than relinquishment of that autonomy.

While the intimate but platonic quality of Frank and Laura's friendship that supposedly characterizes nineteenth-century female relations prepares Laura emotionally and psychologically for marriage, their intimacy also evidences the homoeroticism that sexologists would later argue defines the woman transvestite's inversion. Laura's latent preference for Frank and Frank's reluctance to step aside for Guy suggest that, in a culture typified and controlled by the violent, predatory behavior of its males, the fact "that women seem with special frequency to fall in love with disguised persons of their own sex" (1:95) is not as "noteworthy" as Havelock Ellis later would have us believe. While Mrs. D'Arcy repeatedly places "a slight emphasis on the word friend" (65) when speaking to Laura about Frank, Laura continues to find "very attractive . . . [his] handsome melancholy face" (48), with its "look . . . of perpetual unrest, of yearning" (10). Though Frank uses his voice to defend silenced women, it is his eyes, which shine "with a lustre that Laura had not seen in them before," that register his feeling for Laura. While admitting that he has "not enjoyed anything so much for a long time" (191), the satisfaction that Frank derives from keeping Laura from sexually aggressive men like Swinton evaporates as soon as Guy requests Laura's company. Saying "it is better so" as he looks on with "melancholy eyes" (143), Frank recognizes that he has no right to intervene in a woman's voluntary heterosexuality. Yet Frank fails to register Laura's own ambivalence about Guy's company. She is only "half glad of the exchange" of male escorts and is "haunted" by "the sad hungry look of [Frank's] mysterious eyes . . . for hours afterward" (143). Able to "read [Guy] like an open book" (196), Laura remains "half provoked" (283) by the "big honest fellow" (196). Thus, it is much to Laura's "consternation" (197) that Frank announces that he is going away. As he embraces her and "touch[es] his lips to her cheek," "Laura never thought of resenting the action; indeed she was half-minded to return the caress; Frank seemed so different from other men" (216). Categorically dismissing her abundant signs of interest, Frank sails with the "deep yearning" once again evident in the "gaze" of "his strange eyes" (222).

While Frank attributes Laura's attraction to the success of his transvestitism, it is Rhoda's discovery of his "true" sex that causes Frank to acknowledge the nature of women's attraction to one another. After her sexual liaison with Swinton, Rhoda becomes attached to a working girl, whom she "love[s] . . . with the strength of a passionate nature, concentrating all its affections on one object" (271). Recognizing in Frank's protectiveness over Laura the kind of feeling she has for Maggie, Rhoda alerts him when she uncovers Swinton's abduction plot. In the fervor of his desire to save Laura, Frank inadvertently reveals his "true" sex. "Fascinated strangely" as she watches Frank's "slender figure [and] . . . the movements of [his] slender fingers, as he tossed his papers into some sort of order," Rhoda's face, "pale with a strange wistfulness in her intense gaze," meets Frank's "deep mysterious . . . eyes" and causes him to start visibly as he confronts "in the eloquent earnestness [of her regard] a mute question" (169). It is not until they are both in danger of drowning, as they float in the ocean together holding onto a small piece of their sinking ship, that Rhoda admits that "I know your secret" (277). Already determined to drown in order to ensure Frank's survival, Rhoda asks Frank, "Will you give me a kiss?" (277). As "their cold lips me[e]t in a strange despairing embrace" (277), Frank recognizes both the same-sex desires bound up in yet covered over by the intimacy of female relations and the unique access that his transvestitism gives him to articulating those desires.

Although momentarily "unable to frame a word" (277) after his encounter with Rhoda, once Frank regains his voice he becomes committed to using that voice not only to speak for silenced women but to speak for himself. As the public spokesperson of voiceless women, he continues to vote in elections, but he reacts to Rhoda's words and gesture by devoting his career to articulating publicly his most radical views. In a concise statement of professional purpose, Frank details to Laura the ideal relation between his own voice and the public voice to which his journalistic career gives him access: "I want to be editor-in-chief of some great journal, so that I can conduct it according to my own views, and make it the medium of my own thoughts . . . the experiment has never yet been tried as I hope to try it" (301–2). Frank immediately puts his radical project into practice by confessing to Laura that, while he seems like a brother to her, if she could think of him as a "sister, it would [be] nearer the truth" (364). Though Frank thinks that Laura's interest depends upon his maleness, Laura makes sense of her attraction by arguing that it is based rather on Frank's underlying feminine consciousness. In a statement that simultaneously asserts and neutralizes her homo-erotic attraction, Laura admits, "I thought you were entirely different from any man. . . . I loved you . . . as I might have loved a woman" (365). The "hearty kiss" (364) that Laura gives Frank upon learning that he is a woman signifies and reasserts the sexual innocence of women's bonds in nineteenth-century America. Yet because the women's kiss precedes and so preempts the heterosexual kiss with which the novel closes, it, like Rhoda and Frank's earlier kiss, also acknowledges the political power of women's same-sex desire.

Written before sexological accounts of female inversion firmly placed the woman cross-dresser in "the margins" of American cultural history, *Fettered for Life* shows audiences who read through subsequent sexological paradigms what we least expect: the woman-loving transvestite "in the midst of things, as familiar and crucial as an old friend" (Castle, 3). Yet while this cross-dresser successfully defends many voiceless women with her public speech, it is her extended relationship with another woman that structures the narrative that Blake writes in order to influence public debates over woman's suffrage. Blake's text thus extends our understanding of the persuasive strategies and rhetorical tools that nineteenth-century women used to advocate for the vote. With this expanded model of Victorian woman's suffrage activism, we can suddenly see more clearly the origin, emergence, and political history of the sexological discourse of female inversion that would effectively neutralize the woman's suffrage movement by the early twentieth century. And so, by revealing a rich history of nineteenth-century suffrage rhetoric that depends on the female transvestite, Blake's text and the cultural texts on which it draws compel us to reconsider existing interpretations of women's personal relations and political power in nineteenth- as well as in twentieth-century America.

Conclusion

Women and Political Activism at the Turn into the Twentieth Century

Fifty years after Constance Fenimore Woolson published "The Lady of Little Fishing" in one of the short story collections upon which literary critic Fred Lewis Pattee bases his assessment of her work, he declared that, "during the 'seventies," Woolson "undoubtedly . . . was the most 'unconventional' feminine writer that had yet appeared in America."[1] No doubt because of the unconventionality that, among other things, distinguished Woolson's writing, Henry James considered his friend and correspondent to be "a very intelligent woman" and "gifted authoress" and claimed that, other than William Dean Howells, Woolson was the only English-language novelist he read.[2] However, James was not the only one to voice his opinions. Woolson, in an 1882 letter to James, admits to being confounded by his choice of subject matter in *The Portrait of a Lady*. "How did you ever dare write a portrait of a lady?" she wonders. "Fancy any woman's attempting a portrait of a gentleman! . . . [I]n my small writings, I never dare put down what men are thinking, but confine myself simply to what they do and say" (535). However, what men do and say, as Woolson depicts both in "The Lady of Little Fishing," reveal how their private as well as their public lives depend upon the woman public speaker who enters their community. Written at the end of the era I consider, the short story that many scholars consider to be Woolson's best[3] highlights my project's main premises, showing, first, how discourses about American women's voices and their relation to public speech shape and order a culture in radical transition, second, how women's speech undermines the social change in which it is implicated, and, third, how women writers employ this politically revisionist speech in their fiction in order to contribute to the politics of the public arena. Thus, in her canny, "unconventional" commentary on social transformation and the role women's voices and public speech play within it, Woolson encourages her readers to reconsider the impact of women's voices on American social and political culture.

Threatened by the cultural changes gripping midcentury American society, the male narrator of Woolson's story tries to avoid, but is finally forced to confront and comprehend, them. Indeed, his narrative is an account of that process. On a solitary expedition during the "summer of 1850,"[4] the narrator walks through the woods expecting to encounter the natural world, but instead comes upon a town. Deserted, the "streets, residences, a meeting-house, [and] . . . park" (351) the only indicators of a formerly thriving community, the town appeals to the narrator, and he decides to lodge himself temporarily in the public arena of the meetinghouse. Alone in the abandoned town, the narrator thinks that his will as well as his voice will assume uncontested dominance over both public and private spheres. Addressing the "homes of the past," he sends, from the meetinghouse, his "human voice" (352) ringing through their halls before he begins to tear them down to heat the public rooms in which he resides. Yet the voice of another man soon joins and finally challenges the "brilliant monologue" (354) that the narrator believes indicates his incontestable control over both the town's public and private sectors. Informing the narrator that his knowledge of nature, society, and the influence of each on men is limited, the new arrival compares "the airs of you city gentlemen with your fine guns, improved fishing-tackle, [and] elaborate paraphernalia" with the "hunters of Little Fishing," who waded "through the hard snow, breast high, in the gray dawn, visiting the traps and hauling home the prey" (356). Reflecting American society as a whole, the former town, according to the second narrator, Reuben, was made up of "all kinds of men . . . Scotch, French, English, and American; all classes, the high and the low, the educated and the ignorant; [and] all sorts, the lazy and the hardworking." Yet despite fleeing to "the wilderness to escape the law and ... order" (356) that define society, the men in Little Fishing formed a community that depended upon both because of the influence of a woman preacher. Told amid the town's physical ruin, Reuben's story concerns these men's gradual socialization by a woman public speaker.

It is the woman's, or as the men call her, the "Lady's," speech that creates public order among the unruly inhabitants of Little Fishing. As the Lady walks into the male settlement with its gambling and disorder and begins to preach, her body is spotlighted by the firelight, revealing to the men "her pale face and dove-colored dress, her golden hair" and "tall and slender" body. Confounded by the sight of a woman when "there was not a white woman west of the Sault," the men remain motionless as they listen to her and watch the "wonderful sight [of] that lily face ... that spotless woman standing alone" (360). Her "clear, sweet voice" produces sermons that in turn rely on "no argument, no doctrine, just simple, pure entreaty" (358). Through the tone and delivery of her speech, rather than its content, the Lady attracts the men. Thus, when she asks "for the love of God, my brothers, try to do better," Reuben admits that the men "did try; but it was not for the love of God. Neither did any of us feel like brothers" (358).

However, the order that the woman creates among the men depends upon their careful control over her access to the community. Aware that their intense, competitive desire for the speaking woman threatens their newly ordered community's very existence, the men are forced to protect, rather than indulge in their desire for, her. Because each of the "forty evil-minded, lawless men" who surround the Lady "would have killed his neighbor for so much as a disrespectful thought of her" (360), they are compelled to create a community that "protects" her and by extension themselves from the socially destructive effects of their desire. They thus quickly build a town that carefully marks off public from private space in order to control sexual access to the female body that, despite its relegation to the private arena, remains at the center of their emerging community. Appropriately, the men's first construction project is a stockade that looks "like a miniature fortress" (359), which they build around the Lady's house. Their "own idea," this project creates solidarity among the hitherto hostile, uncooperative men. As Reuben states, "With one accord [they] worked at it like beavers, and hung up a gate with a ponderous bolt inside" (359). Once they restrict access to the female speaker, they devote their efforts to refining the public and other private spaces that emerge within and restructure their society. As Reuben notes, "We took to improving the town. We had lived in all kinds of huts and lean-to shanties; now nothing would do but regular log-houses" (365). Public areas are likewise improved: a public "clearing was soon turfed over like a lawn" and "the whole town burst into blossom" (373).

However, despite the men's efforts, the woman speaker's voice and her body intrude into and undermine the public sphere. The colorless, slender, and almost ethereal body that transfixed the men begins over time to reflect the Lady's unconscious desire. Initially without "color in [her] cheeks," she begins to acquire "a little more hair . . . over the white brow, . . . a faint color in the cheeks, [and] a quicker step." Her voice likewise becomes even "softer, the words at times faltering" (374). As the men listen to the woman orator, they recognize the threat that her sexuality poses to their public order. The town in turn reflects that threat: the grass grows "yellow for want of water, the flowers in the little gardens . . . droop and die, the fountain [becomes] choked with weeds, and the interiors of the houses [are] all untidy" (376). Inquiry regarding the object of her attraction reveals him to be the one man who stands outside the community and its desire. By publicly declaring that the Lady is "a very good missionary, no doubt; but *I* don't fancy woman-preachers" (383), the townsman Mitchell irrevocably isolates himself from the men with whom he lives. Yet in the process, he maintains his vocal and social autonomy both in the story and in its retelling. Expelled from Little Fishing, Mitchell travels alone, but returns to the town thirty years later to recount its history to the "city gentleman" who is ignorant about society and the forces that produce it. As Reuben Mitchell tells his story, his gentleman listener is compelled to reconsider the position of his own voice in the community that the two men establish among the ruins of Little Fishing. Forced to recognize that the "patronizing way" in which he has "talked . . . for two weeks" (366) reflects his mistaken notion that men's public speech is unconnected to the domestic arena and the women within it, the first narrator acknowledges that, because of Reuben's greater knowledge of the society they both flee, their positions are now in fact reversed. Thus, Woolson ends her story with a male character's dawning recognition of the complexity of social life in midcentury America, the vital role women's public speech plays in it, and the implications of both for his own language.

Woolson carefully illustrates how the creation of the public arena as a male domain depends upon the woman speaker and more particularly upon the process through which she is displaced from her natural position in the public sphere. However, the result of this process – the persistent assumption that the public is an essentially male arena – has been difficult to dismantle, not only, as I showed earlier, in linguistic and cultural theory, but in political practice. Thus, the trope of the female voice and its politically subversive public speech that visionary fiction writers created in the nineteenth century in order to alter women's place in the political landscape continued to structure women's critique of their place in American political culture at the end of the nineteenth and well into the twentieth century. For example, in *A Voice from the South* (1892), Anna Julia Cooper advocates for American women's involvement in "every interest that has lacked an interpreter and a defender" by depicting that intervention, like Monk and Phelps did before her, as a process of breaking a repressive, dehumanizing silence.[5] Claiming that the American woman's "cause is linked with that of every agony that has been dumb – every wrong that needs a voice" (122), Cooper contends that "*the world needs to hear her voice*" because it is detrimental to all human beings if "the cry of one-half [of] the human family be stifled" (121). Only "when race, color, sex, [and] condition" – in short, only when "the cause of every man or woman who has writhed silently under a mighty wrong" – is fairly represented in the public arena will "woman's lesson [be] taught and woman's cause [be] won" (125). Almost fifty years later, Dr. Maude Glasgow similarly summarizes women's political situation by commenting that the "desire for better and higher things" that Cooper had ascribed to women's political endeavor still can "not find expression, for woman [is] by force of circumstances inarticulate."[6] Thus, women continue well into the twentieth century to rely on the female voice that I have shown was central to the creation of public and private spheres in order to erode the distinctions between the two.

However, my analysis provides a key to dismantling the persistent association of public with male culture by revealing the important role that the female voice has played in shaping the public arena's enduring identity as a male domain since its inception in nineteenth-century America. My alternative account shows how the female voice in fact became a cornerstone of the public sphere and therefore essential to the diverse discourses that contributed to it. The chapters of this book thus provide us with a new framework for assessing the political contributions that women have made by highlighting in their writing the sociopolitical significance of women's voices and their public speech. From this new vantage point, we can suddenly see how women, throughout the preceding century, effectively represented and advocated for a wide array of ethnic, economic, racial, and gender constituencies. And so, once our "inherited narrative" of American cultural history shifts to accommodate the female voice and its impact on women's diverse acts of public speech, women are able to assume their rightful place as vital contributors to the evolving American political scene.

Notes

Introduction

1. See, e.g., Barbara Welter, *Dimity Convictions: The American Woman in the Nineteenth Century* (Athens: Ohio University Press, 1976), and Nancy Cott, *The Bonds of Womanhood: "Woman's Sphere" in New England, 1780–1835* (New Haven, Conn.: Yale University Press, 1977).
2. Nineteenth-century theories of the female voice remained uncomplicated by other kinds of difference. They thereby reinforced a middle-class culture that claimed representational power for the nation as a whole. However, this book shows how the female voice became a rhetorical device in various political movements that addressed racial, class, and ethnic differences.
3. For general discussion, see, e.g., Mary Ryan, *Cradle of the Middle Class: The Family in Oneida County, New York, 1790–1865* (Cambridge University Press, 1981), and Christine Stansell, *City of Women: Sex and Class in New York, 1789–1860* (New York: Knopf, 1986). For later ramifications, see Alan Trachtenberg, *The Incorporation of America: Culture and Society in the Gilded Age* (New York: Hill & Wang, 1982).
4. Mary Ryan, *Women in Public: Between Banners and Ballots, 1825–1880* (Baltimore: Johns Hopkins University Press, 1990), 131.
5. Ernest Duvergier de Hauranne, *A Frenchman in Lincoln's America* (1864; rpt., Chicago: Donnelley, 1974), 1:285.
6. Robert Oliver, *The History of Public Speaking in America* (Boston: Allyn & Bacon, 1965), 439–42.
7. Many women, of course, reinforced the gender distinction of the public sphere as actively as men.
8. See, e.g., Thomas Gustafson, *Representative Words: Politics, Literature, and the American Language, 1776–1865* (Cambridge University Press, 1992); Michael Kramer, *Imagining Language in America: From the Revolution to the Civil War* (Princeton, N.J.: Princeton University Press, 1992); Oliver, *Public Speaking;* Kenneth Cmiel, *Democratic Eloquence: The Fight over Popular Speech*

147

in Nineteenth-Century America (New York: Morrow, 1990); Gregory Clark and S. Michael Halloran (eds.), *Oratorical Culture in Nineteenth-Century America: Transformations in the Theory and Practice of Rhetoric* (Carbondale: Southern Illinois University Press, 1993); and Philip Gura, *The Wisdom of Words: Language, Theology, and Literature in the New England Renaissance* (Middletown, Conn.: Wesleyan University Press, 1981).

9. Below I discuss at length the important contributions feminist scholars have recently made to this critical conversation by reconsidering and so expanding the definition of public speech.

10. Throughout this project I use the past tense when dealing with historical events, but the present tense when discussing cultural and literary documents because of their ongoing contributions to cultural discourse.

11. See Jürgen Habermas, *On Society and Politics: A Reader,* ed. Steven Seidman (Boston: Beacon Press, 1989), and Hannah Arendt, *The Human Condition* (Chicago: University of Chicago Press, 1958). In Habermas's view the public sphere is defined by and interchangeable with "public discussions that are institutionally protected and that take, with critical intent, the exercise of political authority as their theme" (232). Arendt contends that while action as well as speech contributes to the public sphere's creation, because most political action is "transacted in words," "finding the right words at the right moment" (26) defines political advocacy.

12. See Nina Baym, *American Women Writers and the Work of History, 1790–1860* (New Brunswick, N.J.: Rutgers University Press, 1995), 6.

13. I use the terms "America" and "United States" interchangeably because, while there were multiple ways of defining the nation in the nineteenth century, the emerging middle class, which it is this book's project to track, ignored such differences in order to identify its own values as synonymous with the nation's.

14. This line of inquiry contributes to feminist political theorists' ongoing project of critiquing and revising Habermas's assumption that both the control and the content of public language are the exclusive right of bourgeois men. As Carole Pateman and other scholars have noted, this contention prevents Habermas from assessing the particular interests served by their public debate. For more discussion, see Hanna Fenichel Pitkin, "Justice: On Relating Public and Private," *Political Theory* 9 (August 1981): 337.

15. Baym, *American Women Writers;* Cathy Davidson, *Revolution and the Word: The Rise of the Novel in America* (New York: Oxford University Press, 1986); Lori Ginzberg, *Women and the Work of Benevolence: Morality, Politics, and Class in the Nineteenth-Century United States* (New Haven, Conn.: Yale University Press, 1990); and Christine Krueger, *The Reader's Repentance: Women*

Preachers, Women Writers, and Nineteenth-Century Social Discourse (Chicago: University of Chicago Press, 1992). In addition, see Barbara Bardes and Suzanne Gossett, *Declarations of Independence: Women and Political Power in Nineteenth-Century American Fiction* (New Brunswick, N.J.: Rutgers University Press, 1990); Gillian Brown, *Domestic Individualism: Imagining Self in Nineteenth-Century America* (Berkeley: University of California Press, 1990); Cynthia Jordan, *Second Stories: The Politics of Language, Form, and Gender in Early American Fictions* (Chapel Hill: University of North Carolina Press, 1989); and Joyce Warren (ed.), *The (Other) American Traditions: Nineteenth-Century Women Writers* (New Brunswick, N.J.: Rutgers University Press, 1993).

16. Nina Baym, *Woman's Fiction: A Guide to Novels by and about Women in America, 1820–1870* (Ithaca, N.Y.: Cornell University Press, 1978); Davidson, *Revolution and the Word;* Mary Kelley, *Private Woman, Public Stage: Literary Domesticity in Nineteenth-Century America* (New York: Oxford University Press, 1984); and Jane Tompkins, *Sensational Designs: The Cultural Work of American Fiction, 1790–1860* (New York: Oxford University Press, 1985).

17. Claire Kahane, *Passions of the Voice: Hysteria, Narrative, and the Figure of the Speaking Woman, 1850–1915* (Baltimore: Johns Hopkins University Press, 1995), xiii. Kahane's work, while enriching my own, differs from it significantly. Whereas Kahane's interest centers on the female voice's role in psychoanalysis, my own analysis of the female voice historicizes and contextualizes psychoanalytic paradigms.

18. Feminist scholars often inadvertently perpetuate this notion by assuming that the public sphere is always already coterminous with male identity and that women's public activity poses a challenge to this already established regime only after the fact. However, in this project I analyze how such an association is created and perpetuated in the first place and show the primary role that the female voice plays in such a project.

19. Linda Kerber et al., "Beyond Roles, Beyond Spheres: Thinking about Gender in the Early Republic," *William and Mary Quarterly* 46 (July 1989): 582. I would like to thank the Cambridge University Press reader for directing me to this article.

20. In addition to the texts already cited, see Nancy Armstrong, *Desire and Domestic Fiction: A Political History of the Novel* (New York: Oxford University Press, 1987).

21. See Davidson's *Revolution and the Word* for a rich analysis of the interrelations that characterized nineteenth-century social, literary, and cultural discourses.

22. Because the literature that I analyze not only emerges from, but often continues to be identified with, cultural and historical texts, my separate

assessment of the novels is not an ideological but a practical decision, enabling me to show most clearly how each novel engages in particular political debates.

23. Homi Bhabha, *Nation and Narration* (London: Routledge, 1990), 300.

24. For a complete discussion of the interrelations between slavery and nativism, see Tyler Anbinder, *Nativism and Slavery: The Northern Know Nothings and the Politics of the 1850s* (New York: Oxford University Press, 1992).

25. Camille Roman, Suzanne Juhasz, and Cristanne Miller, eds. *The Women and Language Debate: A Sourcebook* (New Brunswick, N.J.: Rutgers University Press, 1994), 10.

26. Jacqueline Rose, *Sexuality in the Field of Vision* (London: Verso, 1986).

27. Penelope Brown, "Gender, Politeness, and Confrontation in Tenejapa," in *The Women and Language Debate*, ed. Roman et al., 323.

28. Deborah Tannen, *That's Not What I Meant: How Conversational Style Makes or Breaks Relationships* (New York: Ballantine, 1987).

29. Penelope Eckert and Sally McConnell-Ginet, "Think Practically and Look Locally: Language and Gender as Community-Based Practice," in *The Women and Language Debate*, ed. Roman et al., 455.

1. Bawdy Talk

1. *The Writings of Thomas Jefferson*, ed. Andrew A. Lipscomb and Albert E. Bergh (Washington, D.C.: Thomas Jefferson Memorial Association, 1907), 13: 339.

2. Cynthia Jordan, *Second Stories: The Politics of Language, Form, and Gender in Early American Fictions* (Chapel Hill: University of North Carolina Press, 1989), 5.

3. Kenneth Cmiel, *Democratic Eloquence: The Fight over Popular Speech in Nineteenth-Century America* (New York: Morrow, 1990). For accounts of nineteenth-century language and American political culture, also see David Simpson, *The Politics of American English, 1776–1850* (New York: Oxford University Press, 1986); Thomas Gustafson, *Representative Words: Politics, Literature, and the American Language, 1776–1865* (Cambridge University Press, 1992); Dennis Baron, *Grammar and Gender* (New Haven, Conn.: Yale University Press, 1986); and Michael Kramer, *Imagining Language in America: From the Revolution to the Civil War* (Princeton, N.J.: Princeton University Press, 1992).

4. Paula Baker, "The Domestication of Politics: Women and American Political Society, 1780–1920," *American Historical Review* 89, no. 3 (June 1984): 629. Similarly, Nancy Cott's pivotal argument that women's purity or "passionlessness" allowed them unprecedented political interaction has provided the starting point for the work of numerous other scholars of Ameri-

can culture who have consistently shown the political effectiveness that nineteenth-century women derived from moral suasion. See Nancy Cott, " 'Passionlessness': An Interpretation of Victorian Sexual Ideology, 1790–1850," *Signs* 4 (1978): 219–36.

5. Barbara Bardes and Suzanne Gossett, *Declarations of Independence: Women and Political Power in Nineteenth-Century American Fiction* (New Brunswick, N.J.: Rutgers University Press, 1990), 38.

6. I would like to thank one of *American Literature*'s reviewers for this invaluable insight.

7. Arguing either that women orators lost femininity and were considered masculine or that their femininity made them sexually vulnerable once they entered the public arena, the accounts of cultural historians and literary critics have continued to rely upon the links that linguists forged between women's public speech and the unruly sexuality of the women speakers.

8. Sarah J. Hale, *The Lecturess, or Woman's Sphere* (Boston: Whipple & Damrell, 1839), and Henry James, *The Bostonians* (1886; rpt., Harmondsworth: Penguin Classics, 1987). All subsequent references will be to these editions and will be incorporated parenthetically in the body of the text.

9. Otto Jesperson, *Language: Its Nature, Development and Origin* (New York: Henry Holt, 1924), 251.

10. Otto Jesperson, *Growth and Structure of the English Language* (1906; rpt., Leipzig: B. G. Teubner, 1919), 9, 17.

11. Noah Webster, *A Grammatical Institute of the English Language* (1783; rpt., Menston: Scolar Press, 1968), 15.

12. Noah Webster, *A Collection of Essays and Fugitiv Writings on Moral, Historical, Political and Literary Subjects* (1790; rpt., Delmar, N.Y.: Scholar's Facsimiles, 1977), 28.

13. James Fenimore Cooper, *Notions of the Americans: Picked Up by a Travelling Bachelor* (London: Henry Colburn, 1828), 165.

14. Thomas Wentworth Higginson, *Woman and the Alphabet* (1881; rpt., New York: Arno Press, 1972), 33.

15. William Dean Howells, "Our Daily Speech," *Harper's Bazar* 40 (November 1906): 931.

16. Richard Grant White, *Words and Their Uses, Past and Present: A Study of the English Language* (New York: Sheldon, 1870), 63.

17. Richard Grant White, *Every-Day English* (Boston: Houghton Mifflin, 1881), 93–4. Quoted in Baron, *Grammar and Gender,* 74.

18. Henry James, "The Speech of American Women," in *French Writers and American Women Essays,* ed. Peter Buitenhuis (Branford, Conn.: Compass, 1960), 38.

19. Thomas Wilson, *The Many Advantages of a Good Language to Any Nation* (London, 1724; rpt., Menston: Scolar Press, 1969), 37.

20. James Fenimore Cooper, *The American Democrat: Or Hints on the Social and Civic Relations of the United States of America* (1838; rpt., New York: Vintage, 1956), 116.

21. Ellin Devis, *The Accidence: Or, First Rudiments of English Grammar, Designed for the Use of Young Ladies* (London, 1801), 136. Quoted in Baron, *Grammar and Gender,* 58.

22. Henry James, "The Question of Our Speech," in *French Writers and American Women Essays,* ed. Buitenhuis, 27.

23. Sigmund Freud, *Dora: An Analysis of a Case of Hysteria* (1905; rpt., New York: Collier Books, 1963). As the proliferation of feminist discussion about Dora's case history illustrates, Freud's silencing and rewriting of Dora's story has generated compensatory dialogue between otherwise divergent feminisms. For discussion see Charles Bernheimer and Claire Kahane (eds.), *In Dora's Case: Freud – Hysteria – Feminism* (New York: Columbia University Press, 1985); Richard Feldstein and Judith Roof (eds.), *Feminism and Psychoanalysis* (Ithaca, N.Y.: Cornell University Press, 1989); and Richard Feldstein and Henry Sussman (eds.), *Psychoanalysis and . . .* (New York: Routledge, 1990).

24. A notable exception is Helene Cixous, who writes, "Too bad for [men] if they fall apart upon discovering that women aren't men.... But isn't this fear convenient for them? Wouldn't the worst be that women aren't castrated?" See "Laugh of the Medusa," *Signs* 1 (1976): 885.

25. My choice in not capitalizing "symbolic" reflects the project of this essay, which is to dismantle gradually the identification of the symbolic with the phallus.

26. See Deborah Cameron, *Feminism and Linguistic Theory* (London: Macmillan Press, 1985) and *The Feminist Critique of Language* (New York: Routledge, 1990). After pointing out that Lacan offers no explanation for "why the symbolic order is patriarchal," Cameron argues that if semiotic linguistic studies, by assuming that the symbolic is male, unjustifiably deny women access to its main modes of discourse, structural linguistics, including its various forms of feminist structural linguistics, is guilty of the same determinism (*Feminism,* 124).

27. My reliance on James's linguistic attitudes to delineate the limits placed on women's speech is not inconsistent with the following discussion of his treatment of women's speech in *The Bostonians.* Claire Kahane has persuasively argued that James's ambivalence about women's public speech often produces, in *The Bostonians,* hysterical narrative interjections. See her "*The Bostonians* and the Figure of the Speaking Woman," *Psychoanalysis and . . .*, ed. Feldstein and Sussman, 163–75, and "Hysteria, Feminism, and the Case of *The Bostonians,*" in *Feminism and Psychoanalysis,* ed. Feldstein and Roof, 280–98.

28. Judith Fetterley, *The Resisting Reader: A Feminist Approach to American Fiction* (Bloomington: Indiana University Press, 1977), 120.

29. Lynn Wardley, "Woman's Voice, Democracy's Body, and *The Bostonians,*" *ELH* 56, no. 3 (1989): 646.

30. Horace Bushnell, *Women's Suffrage: The Reform Against Nature* (New York: Scribner, 1869), 159.

31. Basil's and William's atypically vehement reaction against women's public speech reveals the power structure that is always present in each text but that remains unacknowledged by the less threatened men.

2. *"Foul-Mouthed Women"*

1. Sacvan Bercovitch, *The Rites of Assent: Transformations in the Symbolic Construction of America* (New York: Routledge, 1993), 253. See also Lawrance Thompson, Foreword to *Pierre: Or, The Ambiguities* (New York: Signet, 1964).

2. Kaja Silverman suggests that "to disembody the female voice . . . liberate[s] the female subject," providing her with "enormous discursive power" and enabling her to talk about "homosexual as well as heterosexual desire." Kaja Silverman, *The Acoustic Mirror: The Female Voice in Psychoanalysis and Cinema* (Bloomington: Indiana University Press, 1988), 186, 164.

3. While numerous scholars have pointed out how domestic fiction manipulates middle-class sensibilities in order to promote political agendas, they have not assessed how domestic fiction might critique its own middle-class biases and ideologies. See, most recently, Shirley Samuels (ed.), *The Culture of Sentiment: Race, Gender, and Sentimentality in Nineteenth-Century America* (New York: Oxford University Press, 1992).

4. Noah Webster, *A Collection of Essays and Fugitiv Writings on Moral, Historical, Political and Literary Subjects* (1790; rpt., Delmar, N.Y.: Scholar's Facsimiles, 1977), 28.

5. Dennis Baron, *Grammar and Gender* (New Haven, Conn.: Yale University Press, 1986), 56.

6. John Pintard, "Letters from John Pintard to his Daughter Eliza Noel Pintard Davidson, 1816–1833," *New York Historical Society Collections* (1937–40), 2: 17. Quoted in Barbara J. Berg, *The Remembered Gate: Origins of American Feminism* (New York: Oxford University Press, 1978), 80.

7. Noah Webster, *A Grammatical Institute of the English Language* (1783; rpt., Menston: Scolar Press, 1968), 2: 15.

8. William Dean Howells, "Our Daily Speech," *Harper's Bazar* 40 (November 1906): 930.

9. Otto Jesperson, *Growth and Structure of the English Language* (1906; rpt., Leipzig: B. G. Teubner, 1919), 240.

10. Otto Jesperson, *Language: Its Nature, Development and Origin* (New York: Henry Holt, 1924), 245.

11. This anecdote regarding American women's use of "limb" rather than "leg" when speaking of pianos is recounted in numerous commentaries on American language. See, e.g., Capt. Marryat, "Language," in *Diary in America, with Remarks on Its Institutions* (London: Longman, Orme, Brown, Green, & Longmans, 1839), 2: 245–7.

12. John D'Emilio and Estelle B. Freedman, *Intimate Matters: A History of Sexuality in America* (New York: Harper & Row, 1988), 166.

13. Reginald L. Cook (ed.), *Ralph Waldo Emerson: Selected Prose and Poetry*, 2d ed. (San Francisco: Rinehart Press, 1969), 15.

14. Herman Melville, *Pierre: Or, The Ambiguities* (1852; rpt., New York: Viking, 1984), and Mrs. Emma D. E. N. Southworth, *The Fatal Marriage* (1859; rpt., Philadelphia: T. B. Peterson, 1863). Critics have consistently associated Melville's novel with Southworth's fictions. However, they have failed to assess the social and linguistic significance of the disembodied female voice in which both novelists are interested. See, e.g., Newton Arvin, "Melville and the Gothic Novel," *New England Quarterly* 22 (March 1949): 41–4, and Bercovitch, *The Rites of Ascent*, 253.

15. While many scholars might identify Lucy and Adelaide as the novel's heroines, my reading suggests that the revisionist work of both texts is conducted by Lionne and Isabel.

16. Walt Whitman to Ralph Waldo Emerson, Brooklyn, August 1856, *Leaves of Grass: Comprehensive Reader's Edition*, ed. Harold Blodgett and Sculley Bradley (New York: New York University Press, 1965), 737.

17. Walt Whitman, *The Primer of Words*, vol. 3 of *Daybooks and Notebooks*, ed. William White (New York: New York University Press, 1978), 746.

18. Walt Whitman, *Other Notebooks, &c. on Words*, vol. 3 of *Daybooks and Notebooks*, ed. William White (New York: New York University Press, 1978), 811.

19. Cook, ed., *Ralph Waldo Emerson*, 128. Quoted in Jesse F. Battan, " 'The Word Made Flesh': Language, Authority, and Sexual Desire in Late Nineteenth-Century America," in *American Sexual Politics: Sex, Gender, and Race since the Civil War*, ed. John C. Fout and Maura Shaw Tantillo (Chicago: University of Chicago Press, 1993), 111.

20. Angela Heywood, "Woman's View of It – No. 2," *The Word* (February 1883). I am indebted to Jesse Battan's " 'The Word Made Flesh' " for introducing me to Angela Heywood's writing.

21. Anthony Comstock, *Traps for the Young*, ed. Robert Bremner (Cambridge University Press, 1967), 158–9. Cited in Battan, " 'Word Made Flesh,' " 117.

22. John C. Spurlock, *Free Love: Marriage and Middle-Class Radicalism in America, 1825–1860* (New York: New York University Press, 1988), 227.

23. Taylor Stoehr, *Free Love in America: A Documentary History* (New York: AMS Press, 1979), 387.

24. Angela Heywood, "The Woman's View of It – No. 3," *The Word* (March 1883).

25. Angela Heywood, "The Grace and Use of Sex Life," *The Word* (June 1890).

26. Angela Heywood, "The Woman's View of It – No. 4," *The Word* (April 1883).

27. Angela Heywood, "Personal Attitudes – Plain Facts," *The Word* (October 1887).

28. Angela Heywood, "Sex Service – Ethics of Trust," *The Word* (October 1889).

29. Angela Heywood, "Seed Forces, Personal and Collective," *The Word* (November 1884).

30. Angela Heywood, "Penis Literature – Onanism or Health," *The Word* (April 1884).

31. Angela Heywood, "Sex-Symbolism – The Attucks Shaft," *The Word* (January 1889).

32. Angela Heywood, "Sex-Nomenclature – Plain English," *The Word* (April 1887).

33. Angela Heywood, "Men, Women, and Things," *The Word* (December 1883).

34. Angela Heywood, "Personal Health – Social Property," *The Word* (September 1887).

35. Angela Heywood, "Men, Women, and Things," *The Word* (October 1883).

36. See Chapter 1.

37. In the first instance see, e.g., Sigmund Freud, *Dora: An Analysis of a Case of Hysteria* (1905; rpt., New York: Collier Books, 1963); Jesperson, *Language;* George McKnight, *English Words and Their Background* (New York: Appleton-Century, 1923); Jacques Lacan, *Écrits: A Selection,* trans. Alan Sheridan (New York: Norton, 1977); and Julia Kristeva, *Desire in Language: A Semiotic Approach to Literature and Art,* ed. Leon Roudiez (New York: Columbia University Press, 1980). In the second instance see, e.g., Mary Daly, *Gyn/Ecology: The Metaethics of Radical Feminism* (Boston: Beacon Press, 1978); Robin Lakoff, *Language and Woman's Place* (New York: Harper & Row, 1975); Dale Spender, *Man Made Language* (London: Routledge & Kegan Paul, 1980); Michael Kramer, *Imagining Language in America: From the Revolution to the Civil War* (Princeton, N.J.: Princeton University Press, 1992); and Carroll Smith-Rosenberg, *Disorderly Conduct: Visions of Gender in Victorian America* (New York: Knopf, 1985). For recent revisionist accounts of language and gender, see Deborah Cameron (ed.), *The Feminist Critique of Language* (New York: Routledge, 1990); Silverman, *The Acoustic Mirror;* and Cynthia Jordan, *Second Stories: The Politics of Language, Form, and Gender in Early American Fictions* (Chapel Hill: University of North Carolina Press, 1989).

38. See, e.g., Mary Ryan, *Womanhood in America: From Colonial Times to the Present* (New York: F. Watts, 1983).

39. See Chapter 1.

40. While temporarily allowing the men to separate the two spheres, women's speech, as I will show, undermines the integrity of both arenas.

41. Susan Warner's *The Wide, Wide World,* published in 1851, was one of the most popular sentimental fictions of the 1850s and to a large extent defined the genre. Novels like Maria Cummins's *The Lamplighter* rework the plot of a young girl abandoned by her family and left to make her way in "the wide, wide world" by herself. Cathy Davidson argues that this plot resonated with female audiences because it so closely described the realities that women faced due to the high mortality associated with childbirth. See *Revolution and the Word: The Rise of the Novel in America* (New York: Oxford University Press, 1986).

42. Though legally fictitious, Pierre's declaration of marriage to Isabel produces the same social effects that a "real" marriage to her would.

43. The homoerotic triangle that Eve Sedgwick identifies among men may apply to the female relations that are established and maintained by heterosexual desire.

44. See Brian Higgins and Hershel Parker (eds.), *Critical Essays on Herman Melville's "Pierre; Or, The Ambiguities"* (Boston, G. K. Hall, 1983), 35, 45, 42.

45. *New York Dispatch* and *Citizen and Gazette.* Reprinted in E. D. E. N. Southworth, *The Fatal Marriage,* ii.

3. Incarnate Words

1. For an analysis of the interrelations between nativism and abolition, see Tyler Anbinder, *Nativism and Slavery: The Northern Know Nothings and the Politics of the 1850s* (New York: Oxford University Press, 1992).

2. *The Sons of the Sires: A History of the Rise, Progress, and Destiny of the American Party and Its Probable Influence on the Next Presidential Election* (Philadelphia: Lippincott, Grambo, 1855), 67.

3. *Awful Disclosures* sold three hundred thousand copies before the Civil War, making it the best-selling book in the United States until *Uncle Tom's Cabin,* and was commonly referred to as "the *Uncle Tom's Cabin* of Know-Nothingism." For more information, see David Bennett, "Women and the Nativist Movement," in *"Remember the Ladies": New Perspectives on Women in American History – Essays in Honor of Nelson Manfred Blake,* ed. Carol V. R. George (Syracuse, N.Y.: Syracuse University Press, 1975), and Barbara Welter, "From Maria Monk to Paul Blanshard: A Century of Protestant

Anti-Catholicism," in *Uncivil Religion: Interreligious Hostility in America,* ed. Robert Bellah and Frederick Greenspahn (New York: Crossroad, 1987), 43–71.

4. R. A. Billington, *The Protestant Crusade, 1800–1860: A Study of the Origins of American Nativism* (New York: Macmillan, 1938), 99.

5. See Welter, "From Maria Monk to Paul Blanshard," 44.

6. Lynn Hunt (ed.), *Eroticism and the Body Politic* (Baltimore: Johns Hopkins University Press, 1991).

7. Jenny Franchot, *Roads to Rome: The Antebellum Protestant Encounter with Catholicism* (Berkeley: University of California Press, 1994), 160.

8. Carleton Beals, *Brass-Knuckle Crusade: The Great Know-Nothing Conspiracy, 1820–1860* (New York: Hastings House, 1960), 46–50. Beals describes one school of thought regarding the text's writing, which argues that Monk dictated, rather than wrote, *Awful Disclosures.*

9. Susan Griffin, "Awful Disclosures: Women's Evidence in the Escaped Nun's Tale," *PMLA* 111 (1996): 93–107.

10. For an account of the innovative rhetorical strategies of nativists, see Donald Zacharias, "The Know-Nothing Party and the Oratory of Nativism," in *Oratory in the Old South, 1828–1860,* ed. Waldo Braden (Baton Rouge: Louisiana State University Press, 1970), 218–33.

11. As Griffin notes, Monk resists describing sexual assault in too great detail in order to retain the narrative authority that accrues to the virtuous women who uphold the nation. She thus identifies herself as a fallen but not dissolute woman.

12. See both Mary Ryan, *Women in Public: Between Banners and Ballots, 1825–1880* (Baltimore: Johns Hopkins University Press, 1990), 27, and Lauren Berlant, *The Anatomy of National Fantasy: Hawthorne, Utopia, and Everyday Life* (Chicago: University of Chicago Press, 1991), 27. Scholarship on nineteenth-century American iconography extends cultural historians' conclusions that women's political activism depended upon the "piety, purity, submissiveness, and domesticity" that Barbara Welter claims defined traditional nineteenth-century American femininity. See Welter, *Dimity Convictions: The American Woman in the Nineteenth Century* (Athens: Ohio University Press, 1976), 21.

13. James Fenimore Cooper, *The American Democrat: Or Hints on the Social and Civic Relations of the United States of America* (1838; rpt., New York: Vintage, 1956), 116.

14. Otto Jesperson, *Language: Its Nature, Development and Origin* (New York: Henry Holt, 1924), 241.

15. William Dean Howells, "Our Daily Speech," *Harper's Bazar* 40 (November 1906): 932–3.

16. Henry James, "The Question of Our Speech" (1905), in *French Writers and American Women Essays,* ed. Peter Buitenhuis (Greenwood, Conn: Compass, 1960), 29.

17. Samuel Busey, *Immigration: Its Evils and Consequences* (New York: DeWitt & Davenport, 1856; rpt., New York: Arno Press, 1969), 40.

18. Maria McIntosh, *Woman in America: Her Work and Her Reward* (New York: D. Appleton, 1850), 122.

19. Anna Ella Carroll, *The Great American Battle: Or, The Contest Between Christianity and Political Romanism* (New York: C. M. Saxton, 1859), 41.

20. Nancy Cott, " 'Passionlessness': An Interpretation of Victorian Sexual Ideology, 1790–1850," *Signs* 4 (1978): 219–36.

21. George Mosse, *Nationalism and Sexuality: Respectability and Abnormal Sexuality in Modern Europe* (New York: Howard Fertig, 1985), 134. In her introduction to *The Invention of Pornography: Obscenity and the Origins of Modernity, 1500–1800* (New York: Zone Books, 1993), Hunt notes that in France the "Catholic clergy were depicted as capable of almost anything" (41).

22. Benedict Anderson, *Imagined Communities: Reflections on the Origin and Spread of Nationalism* (London: Verso, 1983, 1991), 7.

23. See Bennett's "Women and the Nativist Movement" regarding women's membership and role in the nativist movement.

24. Lyman Beecher, *A Plea for the West* (Cincinnati, 1835), 160.

25. "Nunneries Unconstitutional – II," *American (New York) Protestant Vindicator, and the Defender of Civil and Religious Liberty Against the Inroads of Popery,* no. 41 (July 13, 1836), 2–3.

26. Capt. Frederick Marryat, "Diary," in *Diary in America with Remarks on Its Institutions* (London: Longman, Orme, Brown, Green & Longmans, 1839), 1: 78.

27. Michel Foucault, *The History of Sexuality: Volume One, An Introduction,* trans. Robert Hurley (New York: Vintage, 1978).

28. Maria Monk, *The Awful Disclosures of the Hotel Dieu Nunnery* (1836; rpt., Hamden: Archon Books, 1962), 15. All further references will be to this edition.

29. See Welter, "From Maria Monk to Paul Blanshard." Monk's strategy did produce enough concern about the female bodies still within the convent that a search was conducted, but no conclusive evidence was uncovered.

30. William Howitt, "The History of Priestcraft," *Advocate 4,* no. 2 (June 1837): 42.

31. While Rebecca Reed's *Six Months in a Convent* (1835) aroused anti-Catholic sentiment in Boston, Monk's *Awful Disclosures* was, according to Jenny Franchot, "the most widely read convent captivity narrative." See Franchot's *Roads to Rome.*

32. Mary J. Holmes, *The English Orphans; Or, A Home in the New World* (New York: Carleton, 1871), 65.

4. Southern Oratory and the Slavery Debate

1. William Garrott Brown, *The Lower South in American History* (New York: Macmillan, 1902), 125.
2. Virginius Dabney, *Liberalism in the South* (Chapel Hill: University of North Carolina Press, 1932), 80.
3. William Gilmore Simms, "Literary Prospects of the South," *Russell's Magazine* 3 (June 1858), 194. Quoted in Waldo W. Braden, *The Oral Tradition in the South* (Baton Rouge: Louisiana State University Press, 1983), 41.
4. Deborah Garfield, "Speech, Listening, and Female Sexuality in *Incidents in the Life of a Slave Girl,*" *Arizona Quarterly* 50, no. 2 (1994): 19–49; Joanne Braxton and Sharon Zuber, "Silences in Harriet 'Linda Brent' Jacobs's *Incidents in the Life of a Slave Girl,*" in *Listening to Silences: New Essays in Feminist Criticism,* ed. Elaine Hedges and Shelley Fishkin (New York: Oxford University Press, 1994), 146–55; and Gabrielle Foreman, "The Spoken and the Silenced in *Incidents in the Life of a Slave Girl* and *Our Nig,*" *Callaloo* 13, no. 2 (1990): 313–24. Harryette Mullen, "Run-away Tongue: Resistant Orality in *Uncle Tom's Cabin, Our Nig, Incidents in the Life of a Slave Girl,* and *Beloved,*" in *The Culture of Sentiment: Race, Gender, and Sentimentality in Nineteenth-Century America,* ed. Shirley Samuels (New York: Oxford University Press, 1992), 244–65.
5. Thomas Jefferson to Chastellux, September 2, 1785 in *The Portable Thomas Jefferson,* ed. Merrill D. Peterson (Harmondsworth: Penguin Books, 1975), 387–8.
6. Reverend W. Best, *A Dissertation upon Oratory and Philological Inquiry into the Beauties and Defects of the English Language with Thoughts on Preaching and Pulpit Eloquence* (Charleston, S.C.: T. B. Bowen, 1800), 42, 46.
7. Maria McIntosh, *Woman in America: Her Work and Her Reward* (New York: D. Appleton, 1850), 130.
8. The historical sources from which I draw span a period of almost one hundred years, but all comment either retrospectively or immediately on the distinctive characteristics of antebellum oratorical practice.
9. Montrose Moses, *Literature of the South* (New York: Crowell, 1910), 192.
10. George Armstrong Wauchope (comp.), *The Writers of South Carolina* (Columbia, 1910), 42. Quoted in Braden, *The Oral Tradition in the South,* 2.
11. Charles W. Kent, "Southern Literature: A Brief Sketch," in *The Library of Southern Literature,* ed. Edwin A. Alderman and Joel C. Harris (Atlanta: Martin & Hoyt, 1907), 11: 5038.

12. Thomas Watson, *History of Southern Oratory,* in *The South in the Building of the Nation* (Richmond, Va.: Southern Publication Society, 1909), 9: 39–55.

13. Richard Sterling, *Sterling's Southern Orator* (Macon, Ga.: J. W. Burke, 1866), 42.

14. D. Baron Ross, *A Southern Speaker* (n.p., 1856), 306.

15. Anne Firor Scott, *The Southern Lady: From Pedestal to Politics, 1830–1930* (Chicago: University of Chicago Press, 1970), x.

16. George Fitzhugh, *Sociology for the South: Or, The Failure of Free Society* (Richmond, Va.: A. Morris, 1854), 214.

17. Thomas Nelson Page, *Social Life in Old Virginia Before the War* (New York: Scribner's, 1897), 58.

18. Augusta J. Evans to J. L. M. Curry, July 15, 1863, in J. L. M. Curry Papers, Library of Congress. Quoted in Elizabeth Moss, *Domestic Novelists in the Old South: Defenders of Southern Culture* (Baton Rouge: Louisiana State University Press, 1992), 31.

19. Henry Jackson, *The Southern Women of the Second American Revolution: Their Trials and Yankee Barbarity Illustrated* (Atlanta: Intelligencer Steam-Power Press, 1863), 19.

20. Notable exceptions are the Grimke sisters. Their public speech, however, remained unpopular in the South.

21. John Hartwell Cocke to George Fitzhugh 1853, in Clement Eaton, *The Mind of the Old South* (Baton Rouge: Louisiana State University Press, 1967), 11. Quoted in Scott, *The Southern Lady,* 20.

22. Captain J. M. Taylor, Opelousas (La.) *Courier,* August 22, 1868. Quoted in Kathryn Reinhart Schuler, "Women in Public Affairs in Louisiana During Reconstruction," *Louisiana Historical Quarterly* 19 (July 1936): 731, and in Annette Shelby, "The Southern Lady Becomes an Advocate," in *Oratory in the New South,* ed. Waldo W. Braden (Baton Rouge: Louisiana State University Press, 1979), 211.

23. Robert M. Charlton, Address delivered at the commencement of LaGrange Female College, Savannah, Ga., July 1853. Quoted in Eleanor M. Boatwright, "The Political and Civil Status of Women in Georgia, 1783–1860," *Georgia Historical Quarterly* 25 (1941): 301–24; rpt. in *Unheard Voices: The First Historians of Southern Women,* ed. Anne Firor Scott (Charlottesville: University of Virginia Press, 1993), 182.

24. Quoted in Guion Griffis Johnson, *Ante-bellum North Carolina: A Social History* (Chapel Hill: University of North Carolina Press, 1937), 224–58; rpt. in *Unheard Voices,* ed. Scott, 155.

25. Diary of Anne Beale Davis, quoted in Scott, *The Southern Lady,* 10.

26. Caroline Gilman, *Recollections of a Southern Matron* (1839; rpt., New York: Harper, 1850), 256.

27. Thomas Dew, "Professor Dew on Slavery," in *The Pro-Slavery Argument; as Maintained by the Most Distinguished Writers of the Southern States* (Charleston: Walker, Richards, 1852), 339.

28. For discussion regarding the effect of slavery on southern womanhood, see Elizabeth Fox-Genovese, *Within the Plantation House: Black and White Women of the Old South* (Chapel Hill: University of North Carolina Press, 1988); Betty Wood, *Women's Work, Men's Work: The Informal Slave Economies of Lowcountry Georgia* (Athens: University of Georgia Press, 1995); and Philip Curtin, *The Rise and Fall of the Plantation Complex: Essays in Atlantic History* (Cambridge University Press, 1990).

29. Thomas Dew, "On the Characteristic Differences Between the Sexes, and on the Position and Influence of Woman in Society," *Southern Literary Messenger* 1 (May 1835), 498.

30. December 15, 1850, in *Secret and Sacred: The Diaries of James Henry Hammond, a Southern Slaveholder,* ed. Carol Bleser (New York: Oxford University Press, 1988), 213. Quoted in Eugene Genovese, "Toward a Kinder and Gentler America: The Southern Lady in the Greening of the Politics of the Old South," in *In Joy and in Sorrow: Women, Family, and Marriage in the Victorian South, 1830–1900,* ed. Carol Bleser (New York: Oxford University Press, 1991), 128.

31. February 25, 1865, in *Mary Chesnut's Civil War,* ed. C. Vann Woodward (New Haven, Conn.: Yale University Press, 1981), 729.

32. Frederick A. Ross, *Slavery Ordained of God* (Philadelphia: Lippincott, 1857), 106.

33. *North Carolina Standard,* October 22, 1845. Quoted in Johnson, *Ante-bellum North Carolina;* rpt., in *Unheard Voices,* ed. Scott, 153.

34. See Boatwright, "The Political and Civil Status of Women"; rpt. in *Unheard Voices,* ed. Scott, 173–93.

35. *Raleigh Register,* August 26, 1825. Quoted in Johnson, *Ante-bellum North Carolina,* rpt. in *Unheard Voices,* ed. Scott, 152.

36. See Boatwright, "The Political and Civil Status of Women"; rpt. in *Unheard Voices,* ed. Scott, 182.

37. The Section title is from Caroline Lee Hentz, *The Planter's Northern Bride* (1854; rpt., Chapel Hill: University of North Carolina Press, 1970), 318. All further references will be to this edition.

38. *Hillsborough Recorder,* July 27, 1825. Quoted in Johnson, *Ante-bellum North Carolina;* rpt. in *Unheard Voices,* ed. Scott, 162.

39. Sarah J. Hale, *Northwood: Or Life North and South* (1852; rpt., New York: Johnson Reprint Corp., 1970), 406.

40. Harriet Jacobs, *Incidents in the Life of a Slave Girl* (1861; rpt., Cambridge, Mass.: Harvard University Press, 1987), 18. All further references will be to this edition.

41. In both his own home and Linda's grandmother's house, Flint repeatedly forces Linda to be the single audience to his salacious oratory. His manipulation of southern oratorical tradition, as Jacobs asserts, reflects the pervasive practice of slaveholders and thereby complicates and extends our understanding of southern oratorical culture.

5. Partners in Speech

1. Carol Farley-Kessler, *Elizabeth Stuart Phelps* (Boston: Twayne Press, 1982), 50.

2. Susan Albertine, "Breaking the Silent Partnership: Businesswomen in Popular Fiction," *American Literature: A Journal of Literary History, Criticism, and Bibliography* 62, no. 2 (June 1990): 247. Judith Fetterley similarly argues that, while *The Silent Partner* is "essentially a novel about language" (17), the right to speak is as much "a function of class" as of sex (18). Because Perley uses the "class privilege" associated with her voice to silence the mill workers' demands for wage protection, Fetterley concludes that Perley finally becomes "complicit in her own [as well as in the laborers'] silencing." See " 'Checkmate': Elizabeth Stuart Phelps's *The Silent Partner*," *Legacy: A Journal of Nineteenth-Century American Women Writers* 3, no. 2 (1986): 29.

3. Joanne Meyerowitz, *Women Adrift: Independent Wage Earners in Chicago, 1880–1930* (Chicago: University of Chicago Press, 1988), 50.

4. Carroll Wright, *The Working Girls of Boston* (Boston: Wright & Potter, 1889; rpt., New York: Arno Press, 1969), 120.

5. Lillie Devereux Blake, *Report upon the Relations Between Capital and Labor* (1883), 4: 599. Quoted in Alice Kessler-Harris, *Out to Work: A History of Wage-Earning Women in the United States* (New York: Oxford University Press, 1982), 104.

6. Virginia Penny, *Think and Act: A Series of Articles Pertaining to Men and Women, Work and Wages* (Philadelphia: Claxton, Remsen, & Haffelfinger, 1869; rpt., New York: Arno Press, 1971), 21.

7. Caroline Dall, *"Woman's Right to Labor"; or, Low Wages and Hard Work: In Three Lectures, Delivered in Boston, November, 1859* (Boston: Walker, Wise, 1860), 5.

8. See Chapter 3 for a lengthier analysis of female iconography and American nationalism.

9. Mrs. Nemo, *A Series of Appeals: Or Lectures Addressed Not Behind a Curtain to One Unfortunate Man, but to All Men and Their Families* (Albany, N.Y.: J. Munsell, 1863), 19.

10. Helen Campbell, *Prisoners of Poverty: Women Wage-Workers, Their Trades and Their Lives* (Boston: Roberts, 1887; rpt., New York: Garrett Press, 1970), 129.

11. Helen Campbell, *Darkness and Daylight: Or, Lights and Shadows of New York Life* (Hartford, Conn.: Hartford Publ., 1895), 240.

12. Elizabeth Stuart Phelps, *The Silent Partner* (1871; rpt., New York: Feminist Press, 1983), 43. All further references will be to this edition.

6. *"Queer Trimmings"*

1. J. C. Flügel, *The Psychology of Clothes* (London: Hogarth Press, 1930), 207. The title of this chapter is taken from Dorothy Quigley, *What Dress Makes of Us* (New York: Dutton, 1897), vi.

2. Mark Twain, "The Temperance Crusade and Woman's Rights," in *Europe and Elsewhere* (1873; rpt., New York: Harper, 1923), 27.

3. Vern L. Bullough and Bonnie Bullough, *Cross Dressing, Sex, and Gender* (Philadelphia: University of Pennsylvania Press, 1993), 158.

4. My use of the word "invert" reflects sexologists' terminology.

5. Havelock Ellis, *Studies in the Psychology of Sex:* Volume 1, *Sexual Inversion* (London: University Press, 1897), 95.

6. Carroll Smith-Rosenberg, *Disorderly Conduct: Visions of Gender in Victorian America* (New York: Oxford University Press, 1985), 280.

7. Because sexual purity, as Barbara Welter and Nancy Cott show, was the linchpin in the Victorian femininity that proved so politically powerful for bourgeois women, scholars have tended to interpret all expressions of intimacy between women as passionless. For example, while Carroll Smith-Rosenberg admits that "an undeniably romantic and even sensual note frequently marked female relationships" (71) in nineteenth-century America, she quickly concludes that such love was "fully compatible with heterosexual marriage" (59). Untouched by the homosexual desire that would later undermine women's political influence, the passionless but intimate female worlds of the nineteenth century helped to produce, according to scholars, the sexually pure femininity from which women derived their social authority and political power. For a discussion of the cult of true womanhood and the importance of purity for Victorian womanhood, see Barbara Welter, *Dimity Convictions: The American Woman in the Nineteenth Century* (Athens: Ohio University Press, 1976). For a discussion of the political efficacy of bourgeois women's sexual purity, see Nancy Cott, " 'Passionlessness': An Interpretation of Victorian Sexual Ideology, 1790–1850," *Signs* 4 (1978): 219–36.

8. This hesitancy to assess the cross-dressing woman's impact on the political, sexual, and gender consciousness of Victorian America indicates not so much a real as a perceived absence of information. Though cultural historical accounts have obscured Victorian women's sexual longing for men, a woman who desires another woman, as Terry Castle points out, remains

particularly "elusive, vaporous, difficult to spot – even when she is there, in plain view." Terry Castle, *The Apparitional Lesbian: Female Homosexuality and Modern Culture* (New York: Columbia University Press, 1993), 2.

9. For an account of this scholarly impulse, see Judith Roof, *A Lure of Knowledge: Lesbian Sexuality and Theory* (New York: Columbia University Press, 1991), 5.

10. Just as the enduring power of psychoanalysis, according to Jacqueline Rose, derives from its account of "patriarchal culture as a transhistorical and cross-cultural force," so sexological accounts of inversion gain cultural hegemony by denying their own historical specificity. See Jacqueline Rose, *Sexuality in the Field of Vision* (London: Verso, 1986).

11. Since the term "homosexual" still tends to reflect sexological ideology, I have chosen to use "homoerotic" to refer to women's same-sex desires and relations.

12. Thomas Branagan, *The Excellency of the Female Character Vindicated; Being an Investigation Relative to the Cause and Effects of the Encroachments of Men upon the Rights of Women, and the Too Frequent Degradation and Consequent Misfortunes of the Fair Sex* (New York: Samuel Wood, 1807), 14. The title of this section is taken from Branagan's text.

13. Because successful transvestitism afforded immediate if subversive social equality, many suffrage activists, frustrated by their exclusion from the suffrage amendment they helped to pass in 1869, donned Elizabeth Smith Miller's bloomers and often experimented with garments that allowed them to pass as men.

14. Sarah Grimke, *Letters on the Equality of the Sexes and the Condition of Women* (1838; rpt., New York: Source Book Press, 1970), 71.

15. Cited in Aileen S. Kraditor (ed.), *Up from the Pedestal: Selected Writings in the History of American Feminism* (Chicago: Quadrangle Books, 1970), 127.

16. Mrs. Oliphant, *Dress* (Philadelphia: Porter & Coates, 1879), 64.

17. Elizabeth Cady Stanton, *Eighty Years and More (1815–1897)* (1898; rpt., New York: Source Book Press, 1970), 201.

18. Menie Muriel Dowie (ed.), *Women Adventurers: The Lives of Madame Velazquez, Hannah Snell, Mary Anne Talbot, and Mrs. Christian Davies* (London: T. Fisher Unwin, 1893), xx.

19. C. J. Worthington, ed., *"The Woman in Battle": A Narrative of the Exploits, Adventures, and Travels of Madame Loreta Janeta Velazquez* (Hartford: T. Belknap, 1876; rpt. in *Women Adventurers*, ed. Dowie), 5.

20. F. L. Sarmiento (ed.), *Life of Pauline Cushman: The Celebrated Union Spy and Scout* (Philadelphia: Potter, 1865), 34.

21. John Adams Vinton (ed.), *The Female Review: Life of Deborah Sampson, the Female Soldier in the War of the Revolution* (Boston: J. K. Wiggin & Wm. Parson, 1866), 61.

22. S. Emma E. Edmonds, *Unsexed: Or, The Female Soldier* (Philadelphia: Philadelphia Publ. 1864), 156.

23. My choice of the phrase "sexual purity" to denote "heterosexual purity" reflects my argument that nineteenth-century accounts of women's crossdressing, because they occur before sexological discourses of inversion, and twentieth-century accounts of Victorian femininity, because they occur after sexological narratives, fail to register "homosexual purity" as an applicable term.

24. Richard Von Krafft-Ebing, *Psychopathia Sexualis: A Medico-Forensic Study* (1893; rpt., New York: Pioneer, 1939), 399.

25. In 1883 Blake reported on the labor conditions of women wage earners to a congressional committee.

26. David Reynolds, *Beneath the American Renaissance: The Subversive Imagination in the Age of Emerson and Melville* (New York: Knopf, 1988), 357.

27. When speaking generally about Blake's text I use feminine pronouns to refer to Frank Heywood. However, see note 30 for a more detailed account of pronoun treatment during my analysis of the text.

28. The title of this section is taken from Lillie Devereux Blake, *Fettered for Life: Or, Lord and Master* (New York: Sheldon, 1874), 318. All further references will be to this edition.

29. Elizabeth Cady Stanton similarly comments that, after experiencing society's disapproval of her bloomers, "I have never wondered since that the Chinese women allow their daughters' feet to be encased in iron shoes . . . for great are the penalties of those who dare resist the behests of tyrant custom" (204).

30. The title of this section is taken from Quigley, *What Dress Makes of Us*, v. The pronouns that I use to refer to Frank reflect his acknowledged gender in the text. Frank identifies himself as female only at the very end.

Conclusion

1. Fred Lewis Pattee, *The Development of the American Short Story: An Historical Survey* (New York: Harper, 1923), 250.

2. Henry James, *Henry James Letters,* ed. Leon Edel. (Cambridge, Mass.: Harvard University Press, 1980), 3: 28, 150.

3. Pattee considers "The Lady of Little Fishing" in depth, arguing that Woolson's story surpasses Harte's "Luck of Roaring Camp" in its treatment of the woman speaker's desire and is therefore "a model short story" (255, 252).

4. Constance Fenimore Woolson, "The Lady of Little Fishing," in *Castle Nowhere: Lake Country Sketches* (1875; rpt., New York: Garrett Press, 1969), 351. All further references will be to this text.

5. Anna Julia Cooper, *A Voice from the South* (1892; rpt., New York: Oxford University Press, 1988), 122.

6. Dr. Maude Glasgow, *The Subjection of Women and the Traditions of Men* (1940). Cited in Mary Beard, *Woman as a Force in History: A Study in Traditions and Realities* (New York: Persea Books, 1946), 29.

Select Bibliography

Albertine, Susan. "Breaking the Silent Partnership: Businesswomen in Popular Fiction." *American Literature: A Journal of Literary History, Criticism, and Bibliography* 62, no. 2 (June 1990): 238–61.

Alcott, Louisa May. *A Modern Mephistopheles*. 1866. Reprint, New York: Praeger, 1987.

Alderman, Edwin A., and Harris, Joel C., eds. *The Library of Southern Literature*. 13 vols. Atlanta: Martin & Hoyt, 1907.

Anbinder, Tyler. *Nativism and Slavery: The Northern Know Nothings and the Politics of the 1850s*. New York: Oxford University Press, 1992.

Anderson, Benedict. *Imagined Communities: Reflections on the Origin and Spread of Nationalism*. London: Verso, 1983, 1991.

Anderson, Douglas. *A House Undivided: Domesticity and Community in American Literature*. Cambridge University Press, 1990.

Arendt, Hannah. *The Human Condition*. Chicago: University of Chicago Press, 1958.

Armstrong, Nancy. *Desire and Domestic Fiction: A Political History of the Novel*. New York: Oxford University Press, 1987.

Arvin, Newton. "Melville and the Gothic Novel." *New England Quarterly* 22 (March 1949): 41–4. Reprinted in *The Merrill Studies in "Pierre."* Edited by Ralph Willett. Columbus, Ohio: Merrill 1971. 12–15.

Baker, Paula. "The Domestication of Politics: Women and American Political Society, 1780–1920." *American Historical Review* 89, no. 3 (1984): 620–47.

Bardes, Barbara, and Gossett, Suzanne. *Declarations of Independence: Women and Political Power in Nineteenth-Century American Fiction*. New Brunswick, N.J.: Rutgers University Press, 1990.

Baron, Denis. *Grammar and Good Taste: Reforming the American Language*. New Haven, Conn.: Yale University Press, 1982.

Grammar and Gender. New Haven, Conn.: Yale University Press, 1986.

Bate, Barbara, and Taylor, Anita, eds. *Women's Communicating: Studies of Women's Talk.* Norwood, N.J.: Ablex, 1988.

Baym, Nina. *Feminism and American Literary History.* New Brunswick N. J.: Rutgers University Press, 1992.

   Woman's Fiction: A Guide to Novels by and about Women in America, 1820–1870. Ithaca, N.Y.: Cornell University Press, 1978. Reprint, Urbana: University of Illinois Press, 1993.

   American Women Writers and the Work of History, 1790–1860. New Brunswick N.J.: Rutgers University Press, 1995.

Beals, Carleton. *Brass-Knuckle Crusade: The Great Know-Nothing Conspiracy, 1820–1860.* New York: Hastings House, 1960.

Beard, Mary. *Woman as a Force in History: A Study in Traditions and Realities.* New York: Persea Books, 1946.

Beecher, Lyman. *A Plea for the West.* Cincinnati, 1835.

Bennett, David. "Women and the Nativist Movement." In *"Remember the Ladies": New Perspectives on Women in American History – Essays in Honor of Nelson Manfred Blake.* Edited by Carol George. Syracuse, N.Y.: Syracuse University Press, 1975. 71–89.

Bercovitch, Sacvan. *The Rites of Assent: Transformations in the Symbolic Construction of America.* New York: Routledge, 1993.

Berg, Barbara. *The Remembered Gate: Origins of American Feminism.* New York: Oxford University Press, 1978.

Berlant, Lauren. *The Anatomy of National Fantasy: Hawthorne, Utopia, and Everyday Life.* Chicago: University of Chicago Press, 1992.

Bernhard, Virginia, Brandon, Betty, Fox-Genovese, Elizabeth, and Perdue, Theda. *Southern Women: Histories and Identities.* Columbia: University of Missouri Press, 1992.

Bernheimer, Charles, and Kahane, Claire, eds. *In Dora's Case: Freud – Hysteria – Feminism.* New York: Columbia University Press, 1985.

Best, Reverend W. *A Dissertation upon Oratory and Philological Inquiry into the Beauties and Defects of the English Language.* Charleston: T. B. Bowen, 1800.

Bhabha, Homi. *Nation and Narration.* London: Routledge, 1990.

Billington, R. A. *The Protestant Crusade 1800–1860: A Study of the Origins of American Nativism.* New York: Macmillan, 1938.

Bisson, Wilfred. *Countdown to Violence: The Charlestown Convent Riot of 1834.* New York: Garland, 1989.

Blake, Lillie Devereux. *Fettered for Life: Or, Lord and Master.* New York: Sheldon, 1874.

Blatt, Martin Henry. *Free Love and Anarchism: The Biography of Ezra Heywood.* Urbana: University of Illinois Press, 1989.

Bleser, Carol, ed. *Secret and Sacred: The Diaries of James Henry Hammond, a Southern Slaveholder.* New York: Oxford University Press, 1988.

In Joy and in Sorrow: Women, Family, and Marriage in the Victorian South, 1830–1900. New York: Oxford University Press, 1991.

Boyle, Regis Louise. *Mrs E. D. E. N. Southworth, Novelist.* Washington, D.C.: Catholic University of America Press, 1939.

Braden, Waldo. *The Oral Tradition in the South.* Baton Rouge: Louisiana State University Press, 1983.

Braden, Waldo W., ed. *Oratory in the New South.* Baton Rouge: Louisiana State University Press, 1979.

Branagan, Thomas. *The Excellency of the Female Character Vindicated; Being an Investigation Relative to the Cause and Effects of the Encroachments of Men upon the Rights of Women, and the Too Frequent Degradation and Consequent Misfortunes of the Fair Sex.* New York: Samuel Wood, 1807.

Broadhead, Richard. *Cultures of Letters: Scenes of Reading and Writing in Nineteenth-Century America.* Chicago: University of Chicago Press, 1993.

Brooks, Peter. *Body Work: Objects of Desire in Modern Narrative.* Cambridge, Mass.: Harvard University Press, 1993.

Brown, Gillian. *Domestic Individualism: Imagining Self in Nineteenth-Century America.* Berkeley: University of California Press, 1990.

Brown, William Garrott. *The Lower South in American History.* New York: Macmillan, 1902.

Bullough, Vern L., and Bullough, Bonnie. *Cross Dressing, Sex, and Gender.* Philadelphia: University of Pennsylvania Press, 1993.

Butler, Judith. *Gender Trouble: Feminism and the Subversion of Identity.* London: Routledge, 1990.

Bodies That Matter: On the Discursive Limits of "Sex." New York: Routledge, 1993.

Busey, Samuel. *Immigration: Its Evils and Consequences.* New York. 1856.

Cameron, Deborah. *Feminism and Linguistic Theory.* London: Macmillan, Press, 1985.

Cameron, Deborah, ed. *The Feminist Critique of Language.* New York: Routledge, 1990.

Campbell, Helen. *Prisoners of Poverty: Women Wage-Workers, Their Trades and Their Lives.* 1887. Reprint, New York: Garrett Press, 1970.

Women Wage-Earners: Their Past, Their Present, and Their Future. Boston: Roberts, 1893. Reprint, New York: Arno Press, 1972.

Darkness and Daylight: Or, Lights and Shadows of New York Life. Hartford, Conn.: Hartford, 1895.

Campbell, Karyln Kohrs. *Man Cannot Speak for Her: A Critical Study of Early Feminist Rhetoric.* New York: Greenwood Press, 1989.

Caraway, Nancy. *Segregated Sisterhood: Racism and the Politics of American Feminism.* Knoxville: University of Tennessee Press, 1991.

Carby, Hazel. *Reconstructing Womanhood: The Emergence of the Afro-American Woman Novelist.* New York: Oxford University Press, 1987.

Carroll, Anna Ella. *The Great American Battle: Or, The Contest Between Christianity and Political Romanism.* New York: C. M. Saxton, 1859.

Castle, Terry. *The Apparitional Lesbian: Female Homosexuality and Modern Culture.* New York: Columbia University Press, 1993.

Cavell, Stanley. *A Pitch of Philosophy.* Cambridge, Mass.: Harvard University Press, 1994.

Cixous, Helene. "Laugh of the Medusa." *Signs* 1 (1976): 875–93.

Clark, Gregory, and Halloran, S. Michael, eds. *Oratorical Culture in Nineteenth-Century America: Transformations in the Theory and Practice of Rhetoric.* Carbondale: Southern Illinois University Press, 1993.

Cmiel, Kenneth. *Democratic Eloquence: The Fight over Popular Speech in Nineteenth-Century America.* New York: Morrow, 1990.

Cogan, Frances. *All American Girl: The Ideal of Real Womanhood in Mid-Nineteenth Century America.* Athens: University of Georgia Press, 1989.

Comstock, Anthony. *Traps for the Young.* Edited by Robert Bremner. Cambridge University Press, 1967.

Connolly, Paula. "Giving Testimony: Social Reform and the Politics of Voice in Four Nineteenth-Century American Texts." Ph.D. Diss. University of Massachusetts, 1991.

Cook, Reginald, ed. *Ralph Waldo Emerson: Selected Prose and Poetry,* 2d ed. San Francisco: Rinehart Press, 1969.

Cooper, James Fenimore. *Notions of the Americans: Picked Up by a Travelling Bachelor.* London: Henry Colburn, 1828.

    The American Democrat: Or Hints on the Social and Civic Relations of the United States of America. 1838. Reprint, New York: Vintage, 1956.

Cott, Nancy. " 'Passionlessness': An Interpretation of Victorian Sexual Ideology, 1790–1850." *Signs* 4 (1978): 219–36.

    The Bonds of Womanhood: "Woman's Sphere" in New England, 1780–1835. New Haven, Conn.: Yale University Press, 1977.

Curtin, Philip. *The Rise and Fall of the Plantation Complex: Essays in Atlantic History.* Cambridge University Press, 1990.

Dabney, Virginius. *Liberalism in the South.* Chapel Hill: University of North Carolina Press, 1932.

Dall, Caroline. *"Woman's Right to Labor"; or, Low Wages and Hard Work: In Three Lectures, Delivered in Boston, November, 1859.* Boston: Walker, Wise, 1860.

Daly, Mary. *Gyn/Ecology: The Metaethics of Radical Feminism.* Boston: Beacon Press, 1978.

Dannett, Sylvia. *She Rode with the Generals: The True and Incredible Story of Sarah Emma Seelye, alias Franklin Thompson.* New York: Thomas Nelson, 1960.

Davidson, Cathy. *Revolution and the Word: The Rise of the Novel in America.* New York: Oxford University Press, 1986.

Degler, Carl. *At Odds: Women and the Family in America from the Revolution to the Present.* New York: Oxford University Press, 1980.

D'Emilio, John, and Freedman, Estelle B. *Intimate Matters: A History of Sexuality in America.* New York: Harper & Row, 1988.

Devis, Ellin. *The Accidence: Or, First Rudiments of English Grammar Designed for the Use of Young Ladies.* London: n.p., 1801.

Dew, Thomas. "On the Characteristic Differences Between the Sexes, and on the Position and Influence of Woman in Society." *Southern Literary Messenger* 1 (1835).

　"Professor Dew on Slavery." In *The Pro-Slavery Argument; as Maintained by the Most Distinguished Writers of the Southern States.* Charleston: Walker, Richards, 1852.

Dewey, Mary, ed. *Life and Letters of Catharine M. Sedgwick.* New York: Harper, 1871.

Dijkstra, Bram. "The Androgyne in Nineteenth-Century Art and Literature." *Comparative Literature* 26, no. 1 (1974): 62–84.

Dillman, Caroline Matheny, ed. *Southern Women.* New York: Hemisphere, 1988.

Dimock, Wai-Chee. "Pierre: Domestic Confidence Game and the Drama of Knowledge." *Studies in the Novel* 16, no. 4 (Winter 1984): 396–409.

Dowie, Menie Muriel, ed. *Women Adventurers: The Lives of Madame Velazquez, Hannah Snell, Mary Anne Talbot, and Mrs. Christian Davies.* London: T. Fisher Unwin, 1893.

DuBois, Ellen Carol. *Feminism and Suffrage: The Emergence of an Independent Women's Movement in America, 1848–1869.* Ithaca, N.Y.: Cornell University Press, 1978.

DuBois, Ellen Carol, and Ruiz, Vicki, eds. *Unequal Sisters: A Multicultural Reader in U.S. Women's History.* New York: Routledge, 1990.

Eaton, Clement. *The Mind of the Old South.* Baton Rouge: Louisiana State University Press, 1964.

Edmonds, S. Emma E. *Unsexed: Or, The Female Soldier.* Philadelphia: Philadelphia Publ. 1864.

Ellis, Havelock. *Sexual Inversion.* Vol. 1 of *Studies in the Psychology of Sex.* 1897. Reprint, New York: Random House, 1936.

　The Sexual Impulse in Women. Vol. 2 of *Studies in the Psychology of Sex.* 1898. Reprint, New York: Random House, 1936.

Farley-Kessler, Carol. *Elizabeth Stuart Phelps.* Boston: Twayne Press, 1982.

Feldstein, Richard, and Roof, Judith, eds. *Feminism and Psychoanalysis.* Ithaca, N.Y.: Cornell University Press, 1989.

Feldstein, Richard, and Sussman, Henry, eds. *Psychoanalysis and . . . .* New York: Routledge, 1990.

Fetterley, Judith. *The Resisting Reader: A Feminist Approach to American Fiction.* Bloomington: Indiana University Press, 1977.

" 'Checkmate': Elizabeth Stuart Phelps's *The Silent Partner.*" *Legacy: A Journal of Nineteenth-Century American Women Writers* 3, no. 2 (1986): 17–29.

Finck, Henry. *Romantic Love and Personal Beauty: Their Development, Causal Relations, Historic and National Peculiarities.* New York: Macmillan, 1891.

Fitzhugh, George. *Sociology for the South: Or, The Failure of Free Society.* Richmond, Va.: A. Morris, 1854.

Flügel, J. C. *The Psychology of Clothes.* London: Hogarth Press, 1930.

Foucault, Michel. *The History of Sexuality:* Vol. 1, *An Introduction.* Translated by Robert Hurley. New York: Vintage, 1978.

Fout, John C., and Tantillo, Maura Shaw, eds. *American Sexual Politics: Sex, Gender, and Race since the Civil War.* Chicago: University of Chicago Press, 1993.

Fox-Genovese, Elizabeth. *Within the Plantation House: Black and White Women of the Old South.* Chapel Hill: University of North Carolina Press, 1988.

Franchot, Jenny. *Roads to Rome: The Antebellum Protestant Encounter with Catholicism.* Berkeley: University of California Press, 1994.

Freud, Sigmund. *Dora: An Analysis of a Case of Hysteria.* 1905. Reprint, New York: Collier Books, 1963.

Fryer, Judith. *The Faces of Eve: Women in the Nineteenth-Century Novel.* New York: Oxford University Press, 1976.

Fuss, Diana. *Essentially Speaking: Feminism, Nature, and Difference.* New York: Routledge, 1989.

Gaines, Francis Pendelton. *Southern Oratory: A Study in Idealism.* Tuscaloosa: University of Alabama Press, 1946.

Gallop, Jane. *The Daughter's Seduction: Feminism and Psychoanalysis.* New York: Cornell University Press, 1982.

———. *Thinking Through the Body.* New York: Columbia University Press, 1988.

Garber, Marjorie. *Vested Interests: Cross-Dressing and Cultural Anxiety.* New York: Routledge, 1992.

Gilbert, Sandra, and Gubar, Susan. *Sexchanges.* Vol. 2 of *No Man's Land: The Place of the Woman Writer in the Twentieth Century.* New Haven, Conn.: Yale University Press, 1988.

Giles, Paul. *American Catholic Arts and Fictions: Culture, Ideology, Aesthetics.* Cambridge University Press, 1992.

Gilligan, Carol. *In a Different Voice: Psychological Theory and and Women's Development.* Cambridge, Mass.: Harvard University Press, 1982.

Gilman, Caroline. *Recollections of a Southern Matron.* 1839. Reprint, New York: Harper, 1850.

Ginzberg, Lori. *Women and the Work of Benevolence: Morality, Politics, and Class in the Nineteenth-Century United States.* New Haven, Conn.: Yale University Press, 1990.

Gorsky, Susan. *Femininity to Feminism: Women and Literature in the Nineteenth Century.* New York: Twayne, 1992.

Goshgarian, G. M.. *To Kiss the Chastening Rod: Domestic Fiction and Sexual Ideology in the American Renaissance.* Ithaca, N.Y.: Cornell University Press, 1992.

Graddol, David, and Swann, Joan. *Gender Voices.* Oxford: Basil Blackwell, 1989.

Grimke, Sarah. *Letters on the Equality of the Sexes and the Condition of Women.* 1838. Reprint, New York: Source Book Press, 1970.

Gura, Philip. *The Wisdom of Words: Language, Theology, and Literature in the New England Renaissance.* Middletown, Conn.: Wesleyan University Press, 1981.

Gustafson, Thomas. *Representative Words: Politics, Literature, and the American Language, 1776–1865.* Cambridge University Press, 1992.

Habermas, Jürgen. *On Society and Politics: A Reader.* Edited by Steven Seidman. Boston: Beacon Press, 1989.

Hale, Sarah J. *The Lecturess, or Woman's Sphere.* Boston: Whipple & Damrell, 1839.

Haliczer, Stephen. *Sexuality in the Confessional: A Sacrament Profaned.* New York: Oxford University Press, 1996.

Hanaford, Phebe. *Daughters of America: Or Women of the Century.* Augusta, Me.: n.p., 1882.

Harris, Sharon, ed. *American Women Writers to 1800.* New York: Oxford University Press, 1996.

Hauranne, Ernest Duvergier, de. *A Frenchman in Lincoln's America,* 2 vols. 1864. Reprint, Chicago: Donnelley, 1974.

Hennesey, James. *American Catholics: A History of the Roman Catholic Community in the United States.* New York: Oxford University Press, 1981.

Hentz, Caroline Lee. *The Planter's Northern Bride.* 1854. Reprint, Chapel Hill: University of North Carolina Press, 1970.

Heywood, Angela. "The Woman's View of It – No. 2." *The Word* (February 1883).

"The Woman's View of It – No. 3." *The Word* (March 1883).

"The Woman's View of It – No. 4." *The Word* (April 1883).

"Men, Women, and Things." *The Word* (October 1883).

"Men, Women, and Things." *The Word* (December 1883).

"Penis Literature – Onanism or Health." *The Word* (April 1884).

"Seed Forces, Personal and Collective." *The Word* (November 1884).

"Sex-Nomenclature – Plain English." *The Word* (April 1887).

"Personal Attitudes – Plain Facts." *The Word* (October 1887).

"Sex Symbolism – The Attucks Shaft." *The Word* (January 1889).

"Sex Service – Ethics of Trust." *The Word* (October 1889).

"The Grace and Use of Sex Life." *The Word* (June 1890).

Higgins, Brian, and Parker, Hershel, eds. *Critical Essays on Herman Melville's "Pierre: Or, The Ambiguities."* Boston: G. K. Hall, 1983.

Higginson, Thomas Wentworth. *Woman and the Alphabet.* 1881. Reprint, New York: Arno Press, 1972.

Howe, Irving. *Politics and the Novel.* London: Stevens, 1961.

Howells, William Dean. *The Rise of Silas Lapham.* 1885. Reprint, Harmondsworth: Penguin, 1983.

"Our Daily Speech." *Harper's Bazar* (November 1906): 930–4.

Hunt, Lynn, ed. *Eroticism and the Body Politic.* Baltimore: Johns Hopkins University Press, 1991.

The Invention of Pornography: Obscenity and the Origins of Modernity, 1500–1800. New York: Zone Books, 1993.

Irigaray, Luce. *This Sex Which Is Not One.* Translated by Catharine Porter. Ithaca, N.Y.: Cornell University Press, 1985.

Jackson, Henry. *The Southern Women of the Second American Revolution: Their Trials and Yankee Barbarity Illustrated.* Atlanta: Intelligencer Steam-Power Press, 1863.

Jacobs, Harriet. *Incidents in the Life of a Slave Girl.* 1861. Reprint, Cambridge, Mass.: Harvard University Press, 1987.

James, Henry. *The Bostonians.* 1886. Reprint, Harmondsworth: Penguin, 1987.

The Tragic Muse. 1890. Reprint, New York: Viking, 1989.

"The Question of Our Speech." 1905. Reprinted in *French Writers and American Women Essays.* Edited by Peter Buitenhuis. Branford, Conn: Compass, 1960. 18–32.

"The Speech of American Women." 1906. Reprinted in *French Writers and American Women Essays.* Edited by Peter Buitenhuis. Branford, Conn: Compass, 1960. 32–54.

Jefferson, Thomas. *The Writings of Thomas Jefferson.* 20 vols. Edited by Andrew A. Lipscomb and Albert E. Bergh. Washington, D.C.: Thomas Jefferson Memorial Association, 1907.

The Portable Thomas Jefferson. Edited by Merrill Peterson. Harmondsworth: Penguin Books, 1977.

Jesperson, Otto. *Growth and Structure of the English Language.* 1906. Reprint, Leipzig: B. G. Teubner, 1919.

Language: Its Nature, Development and Origin. New York: Henry Holt, 1924.

Johnson, Guion Griffis. *Ante-bellum North Carolina: A Social History.* Chapel Hill: University of North Carolina Press, 1937.

Jordan, Cynthia. *Second Stories: The Politics of Language, Form, and Gender in Early American Fictions.* Chapel Hill: University of North Carolina Press, 1989.

Kahane, Claire. "Hysteria, Feminism, and the Case of *The Bostonians.*" In *Feminism and Psychoanalysis.* Edited by Richard Feldstein and Judith Roof. Ithaca, N.Y.: Cornell University Press, 1989. 280–98.

"*The Bostonians* and the Figure of the Speaking Woman." In *Psychoanalysis and....* Edited by Richard Feldstein and Henry Sussman. New York: Routledge, 1990. 163–75.

Passions of the Voice: Hysteria, Narrative, and the Figure of the Speaking Woman, 1850–1915. Baltimore: Johns Hopkins University Press, 1995.

Katz, Jonathon. *Gay American History: Lesbian and Gay Men in the U.S.A.* New York: Harper & Row, 1976.

Kelley, Mary. *Private Woman, Public Stage: Literary Domesticity in Nineteenth-Century America.* New York: Oxford University Press, 1984.

Kellogg, John. *Ladies Guide in Health and Disease.* New York: n.p., 1882.

Kerber, Linda, ed. *Women's America: Refocusing the Past.* New York: Oxford University Press, 1995.

Kessler-Harris, Alice. *Out to Work: A History of Wage-Earning Women in the United States.* New York: Oxford University Press, 1982.

Knobel, Dale. *Paddy and the Republic: Ethnicity and Nationality in Antebellum America.* Middletown, Conn.: Wesleyan University Press, 1986.

Kraditor, Aileen, ed. *Up from the Pedestal: Selected Writings in the History of American Feminism.* Chicago: Quadrangle Books, 1970.

Krafft-Ebing, Richard Von. *Psychopathia Sexualis: A Medico-Forensic Study.* 1893. Reprint, New York: Pioneer, 1939.

Kramarae, Cheris. *Women and Men Speaking.* Rowley, Mass.: Newbury House, 1981.

Kramer, Michael. *Imagining Language in America: From the Revolution to the Civil War.* Princeton, N.J.: Princeton University Press, 1992.

Kristeva, Julia. *Desire in Language: A Semiotic Approach to Literature and Art.* Edited by Leon Roudiez. Translated by Thomas Gora, Alice Jardine, and Leon Roudiez. New York: Columbia University Press, 1980.

Krueger, Christine. *The Reader's Repentance: Women Preachers, Women Writers, and Nineteenth-Century Social Discourse.* Chicago: University of Chicago Press, 1992.

Lacan, Jacques. *Écrits: A Selection.* Translated by Alan Sheridan. New York: Norton, 1977.

Lakoff, Robin. *Language and Woman's Place.* New York: Harper & Row, 1975.

Looby, Christopher. *Voicing America: Language, Literary Form, and the Origins of the United States.* Chicago: University of Chicago Press, 1996.

Manning, Beverley. *Index to American Women Speakers: 1828–1978.* London: Scarecrow Press, 1980.

Manning, Carol, ed. *The Female Tradition in Southern Literature.* Urbana: University of Illinois Press, 1993.

Massey, Mary Elizabeth. *Bonnet Brigades.* New York: Knopf, 1966.

Matthews, Glenna. *The Rise of Public Woman: Woman's Power and Woman's Place in the United States, 1630–1970.* New York: Oxford University Press, 1992.

McConnell-Ginet, Sally, Barker, Ruth, and Furman, Nelly, eds. *Women and Language in Literature and Society.* New York: Praeger, 1980.

McIntosh, Maria. *Woman in America: Her Work and Her Reward.* New York: D. Appleton, 1850.

McKnight, George. *English Words and Their Background.* New York: Appleton-Century, 1923.

Modern English in the Making. New York: D. Appleton, 1930.

Melville, Herman. *Pierre: Or, The Ambiguities.* 1852. Reprint, New York: Viking, 1984.

Meyerowitz, Joanne. *Women Adrift: Independent Wage Earners in Chicago, 1880–1930.* Chicago: University of Chicago Press, 1988.

Minter, David. *A Cultural History of the American Novel: Henry James to William Faulkner.* Cambridge University Press, 1994.

Monk, Maria. *The Awful Disclosures of the Hotel Dieu Nunnery.* 1836. Reprint, Hamden: Archon Books, 1962.

Moore, R. Laurence. *Religious Outsiders and the Making of Americans.* New York: Oxford University Press, 1986.

Moses, Montrose. *Literature of the South.* New York: Crowell, 1910.

Moss, Elizabeth. *Domestic Novelists in the Old South: Defenders of Southern Culture.* Baton Rouge: Louisiana State University Press, 1992.

Mosse, George. *Nationalism and Sexuality: Respectability and Abnormal Sexuality in Modern Europe.* New York: Howard Fertig, 1985.

Müller, Max. *Science of Language.* London: Longman, Green, Longman, and Roberts, 1862.

Nemo, Mrs. *A Series of Appeals: Or, Lectures Addressed Not Behind a Curtain to One Unfortunate Man, but to All Men and Their Families.* Albany N.Y.: J. Munsell, 1863.

Noll, Mark, ed. *Religion and American Politics: From the Colonial Period to the 1980s.* New York: Oxford University Press, 1990.

Oliphant, Mrs. *Dress.* Philadelphia: Porter & Coates, 1879.

Oliver, Robert. *The History of Public Speaking in America.* Boston: Allyn & Bacon, 1965.

Page, Thomas Nelson. *Social Life in Old Virginia Before the War.* New York: Scribner's, 1897.

Papashvily, Helen. *All the Happy Endings: A Study of the Domestic Novel in America, the Women Who Wrote it, the Women Who Read it, in the Nineteenth Century.* New York: Harper, 1956.

Pateman, Carol. *The Sexual Contract.* Stanford, Calif.: Stanford University Press, 1985.

The Disorder of Women: Democracy, Feminism, and Political Theory. Cambridge, Mass.: Polity Press, 1989.

Penny, Virginia. *Think and Act: A Series of Articles Pertaining to Men and Women, Work and Wages.* 1869. Reprint, New York: Arno Press, 1971.

  How Women Can Make Money, Married or Single. Springfield, Mass: D. E. Fisk, 1870. Reprint, New York: Arno Press, 1971.

Phelps, Elizabeth Stuart. *The Silent Partner.* 1871. Reprint, New York: Feminist Press, 1983.

Pickering, John. *A Vocabulary or Collection of Words and Phrases Which Have Been Supposed to be Peculiar to the United States of America.* Boston: Cummings & Hillard, 1816. Reprint, New York: Burt Franklin Reprints, 1974.

Pitkin, Hanna Fenichel. "Justice: On Relating Public and Private." *Political Theory* 9 (August 1981): 337.

Pond, Major J. B. *Eccentricities of Genius: Memories of Famous Men and Women of the Platform and Stage.* New York: G. W. Dillingham, 1900.

Quigley, Dorothy. *What Dress Makes of Us.* New York: Dutton, 1897.

Roman, Camille, Juhasz, Suzanne, and Miller, Cristanne, eds. *The Women and Language Debate: A Sourcebook.* New Brunswick, N.J.: Rutgers University Press, 1994.

Roof, Judith. *A Lure of Knowledge: Lesbian Sexuality and Theory.* New York: Columbia University Press, 1991.

Rose, Jacqueline. *Sexuality in the Field of Vision.* London: Verso, 1986.

Ross, Frederick A. *Slavery Ordained of God.* Philadelphia: Lippincott, 1857.

Rush, James. *The Philosophy of the Human Voice Embracing Its Physiological History.* Philadelphia: Grigg & Elliott, 1833.

Ryan, Mary. *Cradle of the Middle Class: The Family in Oneida County, New York, 1790–1865.* Cambridge University Press, 1981.

  Women in Public: Between Banners and Ballots, 1825–1880. Baltimore: Johns Hopkins University Press, 1990.

Sala, George, ed. *Belle Boyd in Camp and Prison, Written by Herself.* New York: Blelock, 1865.

Samuels, Shirley, ed. *The Culture of Sentiment: Race, Gender, and Sentimentality in Nineteenth-Century America.* New York: Oxford University Press, 1992.

Sanchez-Eppler, Karen. *Touching Liberty: Abolition, Feminism, and the Politics of the Body.* Berkeley: University of California Press, 1993.

Sarmiento, F. L., ed. *Life of Pauline Cushman: The Celebrated Union Spy and Scout.* Philadelphia: Potter, 1865.

Scott, Anne Firor. *The Southern Lady: From Pedestal to Politics, 1830–1930.* Chicago: University of Chicago Press, 1970.

Scott, Anne Firor, ed. *Unheard Voices: The First Historians of Southern Women.* Charlottesville: University of Virginia Press, 1993.

Seidel, Kathryn Lee. *The Southern Belle in the American Novel.* Tampa: University of South Florida Press, 1985.

Silverman, Kaja. *The Acoustic Mirror: The Female Voice in Psychoanalysis and Cinema.* Bloomington: Indiana University Press, 1988.

Simkins, Francis Butler, and Patton, James Welch. *The Women of the Confederacy.* Richmond, Va.: Garrett & Massie, 1936.

Simms, William Gilmore. "Literary Prospects of the South." *Russell's Magazine* 3 (1858).

Simpson, David. *The Politics of American English, 1776–1850.* New York: Oxford University Press, 1986.

Smith-Rosenberg, Carroll. *Disorderly Conduct: Visions of Gender in Victorian America.* New York: Oxford University Press, 1985.

Snitow, Ann, Stansell, Christine, and Thompson, Sharon, eds. *Powers of Desire: The Politics of Sexuality.* New York: Monthly Review Press, 1983.

The Sons of the Sires: A History of the Rise, Progress, and Destiny of the American Party and Its Probable Influence on the Next Presidential Election. Philadelphia: Lippincott, Grambo, 1855.

Southworth, E. D. E. N. *The Fatal Marriage.* Philadelphia: T. B. Peterson 1863.

Spender, Dale. *Man Made Language.* London: Routledge & Kegan Paul, 1980.

Spurlock, John. C. *Free Love: Marriage and Middle-Class Radicalism in America, 1825–1860.* New York: New York University Press, 1988.

Stansell, Christine. *City of Women: Sex and Class in New York, 1789–1860.* New York: Knopf, 1986.

Stanton, Elizabeth Cady. *Eighty Years and More (1815–1897).* 1898. Reprint, New York: Source Book Press, 1970.

Sterling, Richard. *Sterling's Southern Orator.* Macon, Ga.: J. W. Burke, 1866.

Stoehr, Taylor. *Free Love in America: A Documentary History.* New York: AMS Press, 1979.

Sundquist, Eric. *To Wake the Nations: Race in the Making of American Literature.* Cambridge, Mass.: Harvard University Press, 1993.

Sweet, Leonard. *The Minister's Wife: Her Role in Nineteenth-Century American Evangelicism.* Philadelphia: Temple University Press, 1983.

Tannen, Deborah. *That's Not What I Meant: How Conversational Style Makes or Breaks Relationships.* New York: Ballantine, 1987.

Thorne, Barrie, Kramarae, Cheris, and Henley, Nancy, eds. *Language, Gender, and Society.* Rowley, Mass.: Newbury House, 1983.

Tompkins, Jane. *Sensational Designs: The Cultural Work of Amerian Fiction, 1790–1860.* New York: Oxford University Press, 1985.

Trachtenberg, Alan. *The Incorporation of America: Culture and Society in the Gilded Age.* New York: Hill & Wang, 1982.

Twain, Mark. "The Temperance Crusade and Woman's Rights." In *Europe and Elsewhere.* New York: Harper, 1923.

Veeser, H. Aram, ed. *The New Historicism.* New York: Routledge, 1989.

Vinton, John Adams, ed. *The Female Review: Life of Deborah Sampson, the Female Soldier in the War of the Revolution*. Boston: J. K. Wiggin & W. Parson, 1866.

Walker, Mary. *Unmasked, or the Science of Immortality*. Philadelphia: William H. Boyd, 1878.

Wardley, Lynn. "Woman's Voice, Democracy's Body, and *The Bostonians*." *ELH* 56, no. 3 (1989): 639–65.

Warhol, Robyn. *Gendered Interventions: Narrative Discourse in the Victorian Novel*. New Brunswick, N.J.: Rutgers University Press, 1989.

Warren, Joyce, ed. *The (Other) American Traditions: Nineteenth-Century Women Writers*. New Brunswick, N.J.: Rutgers University Press, 1993.

Watson, Thomas. *The South in the Building of the Nation*. 12 vols. Richmond, Va.: Southern Publication Society, 1909.

Webster, Noah. *A Grammatical Institute of the English Language*. 2 vols. 1783. Reprint, Menston: Scolar Press, 1968.

A Collection of Essays and Fugitiv Writings on Moral, Historical, Political, and Literary Subjects. 1790. Reprint, Delmar, N.Y.: Scholar's Facsimiles, 1977.

Welter, Barbara. *Dimity Convictions: The American Woman in the Nineteenth Century*. Athens: Ohio University Press, 1976.

"From Maria Monk to Paul Blanshard: A Century of Protestant Anti-Catholicism." In *Uncivil Religion: Interreligious Hostility in America*. Edited by Robert Bellah and Frederick Greenspahn. New York: Crossroad, 1987. 43–71.

White, Richard Grant. *Words and Their Uses, Past and Present: A Study of the English Language*. New York: Sheldon, 1870.

Every-Day English. Boston: Houghton Mifflin, 1881.

Whitman, Walt. *Other Notebooks, &c. on Words*. In vol. 3 of *Daybooks and Notebooks*. Edited by William White. New York: New York University Press, 1978

The Primer of Words. In vol. 3 of *Daybooks and Notebooks*. Edited by William White. New York: New York University, 1978.

Leaves of Grass: Comprehensive Reader's Edition. Edited by Harold Blodgett and Sculley Bradley. New York: New York University Press, 1965.

Wilson, Thomas. *The Many Advantages of a Good Language to Any Nation*. London, 1724. Reprint, Menston: Scolar Press, 1969.

Wilt, Judith. "Desperately Seeking Verena: A Resistant Reading of *The Bostonians*." *Feminist Studies* 13, no. 2 (1987): 293–316.

Winslow, Rev. Hubbard, and Sanford, Mrs. John. *The Lady's Manual of Moral and Intellectual Culture*. New York: n.p., 1854.

Witt, Linda, Paget, Karen, and Matthews, Glenna. *Running as a Woman: Gender and Power in American Politics*. New York: Free Press, 1994.

Wood, Betty. *Women's Work, Men's Work: The Informal Ecnomics of Low Country Georgia*. Athens: University of Georgia Press, 1995.

Woodward, C. Vann, ed. *Mary Chesnut's Civil War.* New Haven, Conn.: Yale University Press, 1981.

Woolson, Constance Fenimore. *Castle Nowhere: Lake Country Sketches.* New York: Garrett Press, 1969.

Worthington, C. J., ed. *"The Woman in Battle": A Narrative of the Exploits, Adventures, and Travels of Madame Loreta Janeta Velazquez.* Hartford, Conn.: T. Belknap, 1876.

Wright, Carroll. *The Working Girls of Boston.* 1889. Reprint, New York: Arno Press, 1969.

Yellin, Jean Fagan. *Women and Sisters: The Antislavery Feminists in American Culture.* New Haven, Conn.: Yale University Press, 1989.

Index

CAMBRIDGE STUDIES IN AMERICAN LITERATURE AND CULTURE

(*Continued from the front of the book*)